In *The Majesty of God*, Walter Kaiser digs deep into the message of Job, shifting our focus from the pain and tragedies of life to the pure worship and true love of God. This guide provides a valuable framework of reflection for those seeking to learn more about how God reveals himself through suffering. Walt Kaiser, whom I have known for many years, writes with a pastor's heart, a scholar's mind and an unquestionable love for the Bible. If you are teaching or studying Job, don't do it without his book beside you.

Barry H. Corey
President of Biola University and author of *Love Kindness: Discover the Power of a Forgotten Christian Virtue*

Based on a lecture series given at the Billy Graham Training Center, eminent Old Testament scholar Walter Kaiser draws critical spiritual lessons for us all from the debate between Job and his friends, about God's character, His grace and offer of redemption from our sin. My favorite parts of the book are Kaiser's Questions for Reflection and Discussion at the end of each chapter. Kaiser has a gift for getting us to think deeply about the most important issues of life.

Hugh Ross
Astronomer, pastor, president of Reasons To Believe, and author of 17 books on creation

Walter C. Kaiser's commentary on Job is a superb exposition, which offers many insights from the Hebrew text and which helpfully clarifies the differences in the expostulations of Job's four critics. The commentary highlights the continuing relevance of Job's message for those who are experiencing suffering and who are like Job tempted to question God.

Edwin M. Yamauchi
Professor of History Emeritus, Miami University

Job may be the oldest book in the Bible, but in this highly accessible commentary Walt Kaiser makes the ancient story of suffering come alive for our times. He lucidly demonstrates that in the story it is not Job who is on trial, but 'God who is on trial.' And God in his grace comes out of the trial in majestic victory. Highly recommended for pastors and laity.

Dennis Hollinger
President & Colman M Mockler Distinguished Professor of Christian Ethics, Gordon-Conwell Theological Seminary, South Hamilton, MA

THE **MAJESTY** OF **GOD** IN THE MIDST OF **INNOCENT** SUFFERING

THE MESSAGE OF **JOB**

WALTER C. KAISER JR.

CHRISTIAN
FOCUS

Copyright © Walter C. Kaiser Jr. 2019

paperback ISBN 978-1-5271-0304-7
epub ISBN 978-1-5271-0377-1
mobi ISBN 978-1-5271-0378-8

First published in 2019
by
Christian Focus Publications Ltd,
Geanies House, Fearn, Ross-shire,
IV20 1TW, Scotland
www.christianfocus.com

A CIP catalogue record for this book is available from the British Library.

Cover design by Kent Jensen

Printed and bound by
Bell & Bain, Glasgow.

Contents

Preface

This series of lectures was first given at the Billy Graham Cove Training Center in Asheville, North Carolina in June 2018, before an audience that came from some two dozen states and countries. God used this time to bless all of us as we attended to what the Spirit of God was saying to us in our day and in our times. I was much aware of many who had prayed for this time of ministry, for the Lord was near at hand as I spoke.

I am also grateful to my second son Brian Addison Kaiser for drawing up the PowerPoint slides that were used with these lectures. Once again, I am indebted to Christian Focus Publications, Ltd., under the wise leadership of Willie Mackenzie for undertaking the publication of this work and Irene Roberts for typesetting. I am also most grateful to Anne Norrie for her careful work in editing this volume and making it a better read. May our Lord use this work to His honor and glory.

Introduction to Job

Job is placed first among the five poetical books in the Old Testament – followed by Psalms, Proverbs, Ecclesiastes, and the Song of Solomon – which are usually referred to as the 'Wisdom Books' of the Bible. These books not only contain the wisdom of God for mortals, but they reflect on the joy, sorrow, and issues of life arising from all the emotions of human experience. In the book of Job, however, feelings of grief, misery, sorrow, and distress are played out against the backdrop of a man resolute in his claim of his innocence of the accusations brought by three of his alleged friends of being an unrepentant sinner. These three 'comforters' provide no respite or comfort at all to Job! The book quickly shifts the area of its focus away from the losses and suffering of Job to his controversy with his three 'friends' and their thesis that the reason for his suffering is because of his unconfessed sin. In the meantime, God was using these three 'comforters' to do another divine work of grace in Job's life even though apparently neither Job nor the three of them were specifically aware of it as it transpired.

That divine work of grace is a critically important point if we are to successfully interpret the book of Job!

JOB'S NAME

This book gets its name from the main character in the book rather than from its author. The original disyllabic Hebrew name *'Iyyov'* became 'Job' in Latin and English renderings of the Hebrew name. The meaning of this name is uncertain, for some connect it to the Hebrew root *'yb*, meaning 'enemy,' or 'enmity,' while others connect it to the Arabic root *'wb*, meaning 'return,' 'repent,' or 'the penitent one.' The name of Job has been found in the Egyptian Execration Texts from around 2000 B.C. and in the Mari, Alalakh, and Amarna tablets from early second millennium to fourteen century B.C. times.

THE BOOK OF JOB

The book of Job has often been heralded as a masterpiece unequalled in all literature. Martin Luther, for example, assessed Job as being 'magnificent and sublime as no other book of Scripture.'[1] Bishop Lowth, who pioneered work in Hebrew Poetry, said that Job stood as 'single and unparalleled in the Sacred Volume.'[2] Thomas Carlyle opined, 'A noble book; [an] all men's book! It is our first, oldest statement of the never-ending Problem, – man's destiny, and God's ways with him here in this earth ... There is nothing written, I think, in the Bible or out of

---

1. James Strahan, *The Book of Job Interpreted*, Edinburgh: T & T Clark (1913): 28.

2. Robert Lowth, *Lectures on the Sacred Poetry of the Hebrews*, 2 vols., (1787, reprinted 1969) Hildesheim, W Ger., Georg Olms Verlag, 2:347.

it, of equal literary merit.'[3] Even the nineteenth century French writer Victor Hugo eulogized Job by saying it was perhaps the greatest masterpiece of the human mind. One must also see the engravings of William Blake to feel the impact that this book has made on the culture.

Job is also known for the richness of its vocabulary. Job has some 110 words that are found nowhere else in the Bible (called *hapax legomena*). It also has five different words for 'lions' (4:10-11), six separate words for 'traps' (18-10) and six different words for 'darkness' (3:4-6; 10:21-22). It is one amazing book!

Job also has an A-B-A literary form that is made up of a *prose* prologue (chapters 1–2) and epilogue (42:7-17), with a central section (3:1–42:6) written in *poetic* form that contains the speeches of Job's three friends (Eliphaz, Bildad, and Zophar) with a fourth young man named Elihu (32–37) added later on. Finally the book concludes with the deep searching questions raised by Yahweh to humble proud Job (38–41).

Some have tried to depict Job as a 'drama,' while others have labelled it as an 'epic chorus,' or even as being similar to the dialogues of Plato, but none of these suggestions seem to fit the evidence found in the book of Job, nor have they been accepted by other scholars. There is also a passing similarity, once in a while, to some examples found in the ancient Egyptian and Mesopotamian literature such as: the third millennium B.C. Egyptian text of '*The Debate of a Man with his Soul,*' the 1800 B.C. '*Tale of the*

---

3. Thomas Carlyle, 'The Hero as a Prophet,' *On Heroes, Hero-Worship and the Heroic in History*, ed. Archibald MacMechan, Boston: Ginn, 1901, pp. 55-56.

Eloquent Peasant,' or '*The Babylonian Job*' from the Cassite period of c. 1600 – 1150 B.C. But here too there are many dis-similarities that keep us from providing a pattern that would be a key to the literary style of Job.

Even though the larger part of this book is in poetry, the story of Job is a recounting of the life of a man who actually lived. Most of the Jewish scholars of the Torah consider Job to have been a real historical figure. Likewise, the larger part of Evangelical Scholars agree with this claim of historicity for the book of Job and its central character, for in Ezekiel 14:14 and 20, Job is treated as an historical character of surpassing righteousness and faithfulness to God, along with Noah and Daniel. The New Testament also refers to Job in the epistle of James 5:11 – 'You have heard of Job's perseverance and have seen what the Lord finally brought about.' Therefore, Job is treated in the Bible as one who really existed and experienced these trials.

THE CANONICITY OF JOB

Job is usually placed at the head of the wisdom or poetical books of the Bible, just as *Codex Vaticanus* arranges them. However, there is a wide variety of other arrangements seen in other collections: Job is placed after Deuteronomy in the *Syriac Peshitta* and the *Codex Sinaiticus*. In the Jewish *Baba Bathra* 14b it is located before Proverbs, but after Proverbs in *The New Jewish Publication Society* version. In the Hebrew text of the Old Testament, it appears after Psalms. Thus there is no canonical order for Job that is preferred.

As a wisdom book, it shares many features with such wisdom Psalms as Psalm 1, 19, 37, 73, and 119. Yet when

Job is viewed as a lament, it shares features with such lament Psalms as Psalm 6, 7, 22, 35, 90, 137 and the book of Lamentations. There also are many features in Job which remind us of the patriarchal chapters of Genesis 12–35. In those sections in Job where the language rises to heights of grand expression, especially about God, we are reminded of the sublimity that describes God's majesty, similar to that found in Isaiah 40-66. Job is a book of many modes and exalted speech about God and His deeds.

Among the Qumran Dead Sea Scrolls, it is worth noting that only the books of the Pentateuch and the book of Job are written in what is called Paleo-Hebrew, which is an archaized type of script no doubt intended to indicate that these books were among the oldest compositions in the DSS community. This older type of text may also be on account of the fact that Jewish tradition associated the first five books of the Old Testament and the book of Job with Moses (*Baba Bathra* and the *Syriac Peshitta*).[4]

THE DATE OF JOB'S BOOK

If the question is 'When did the events in the story of Job take place?' or 'When was the book written?' no one is able to answer those questions from a historical or archaeological basis. There are a number of indications, however, that the book was written somewhere close to the patriarchal age of Abraham, Isaac, and Jacob, i.e., from around 2100 to 1900 B.C. For example, Job may have lived to be somewhere around 200 years old, which

---

4. K. A. Mathews, 'The Background of the Paleo-Hebrew Texts at Qumran,' *The Word of the Lord Shall God Forth*, Philadelphia, ASOR, 1983, p. 555.

would compare well with the longevity of the patriarch Abraham's father Terah, who died at the age of 205. The reasoning for such an age goes like this: if Job was about sixty years old when his ten children died, as we surmise, and he lived another 140 years as Job 42:16 informs us, he would have achieved about the same number of years as Terah. Job was also rich in livestock (Job 1:3; 42:12), which accords well with the wealth of Abraham (Gen. 12:16; 13:2) and Jacob (Gen. 30:43; 32:5). Job also was the priest in his family (1:5), suggesting that the priesthood in Israel had not yet been established by this date. In fact, there is no reference in Job to the Tabernacle, the Mosaic laws, or the special festival days. Moreover, the divine name '*Shaddai*' is used in Job 31 times, whereas it is used in the rest of the Old Testament only 17 times. The Hebrew word for 'piece of money' (42:11) is used elsewhere in the Old Testament only two times (Gen. 33:19; Josh. 24:32). These arguments, along with others, led the Jewish scholar Nahum Sarna to conclude: 'The patriarchal setting must be regarded as genuine,'[5] Job, therefore, must be one of the oldest books of the Bible.

GEOGRAPHY AND CULTURE

Wisdom Literature usually does not give a lot of place names in its corpus, so we are limited to a very few indicators that may tell us where and when the book was completed. For example, 'the land of Uz' was the home of Job, but where was Uz? Since its location is uncertain, we must try

---

5. Nahum M Sarna, 'Epic Substratum of the Prose of Job,' *Journal of Biblical Literature*, Vol. 76. 1957, p 25.

to use other approaches to this question. For example, 'Uz' was the name for three persons in the Bible: Aram's son, grandson of Shem (Gen. 10:22); Abraham's nephew, son of Nahor and Micah (Gen. 22:21); and an Edomite who lived in Seir, one of Dishan's sons (Gen. 36:28). This last named man may well have been the one who gave his name to the land of Uz, which we surmise may have been in northern Saudi Arabia, or in Southern Jordan, called in those days Edom. Lamentations 4:21 has Uz in parallel form with the territory of Edom, and Jeremiah 25:20 mentions the 'kings of Uz,' who will be forced to drink the cup of Yahweh's wrath along with Edom, Moab, and Ammon.

Robert Alden[6] suggests that the best candidate for the land of Uz is the Wadi Sirhan, a depression running for some two hundred miles long from northwest (near Zarqa) towards the southeast (near Jawf). There the waters that ran off Jebel Druz flowed into that depression. Therefore, this area was capable of supporting such large herds as Job possessed. This catchment basin for runoff water was located mainly in the northwestern part of Saudi Arabia, yet it was close enough to Edom to be linked with that country as well.

THE CONTEST FOUND IN JOB

As the book of Job opens, we, the readers of this book, are given some program notes to help us understand the book – explanations that not even Job is aware of. Here in this opening scene, we are given a brief glimpse of what

6. Robert L. Alden, *The New American Commentary: An Exegetical and Theological Exposition of the Scripture: Job,* vol 11, (Nashville: Broadman and Holman, 1993, p 47.

is involved in answering the eternal question: 'Why do mortals suffer?' We will learn that the answers to this question are not as simplistic as many assume, but we see a whole new order of thinking and learning from the hand of a gracious Lord.

The book begins with a heavenly consultation in which God is conferring with His angelic creation in the celestial realm; however, among these angels Satan is surprisingly, but defiantly present. Satan has just returned from traversing back and forth throughout the whole earth. He defiantly throws on the table his challenge to God, no less, asserting: 'Humans love you out of self-interest, i.e. because you bless them so richly. But take away those blessings and they will curse you to your face.' Satan has thrown down the challenge; what was the Lord to do about such effrontery or just plain *chutzpah* on Satan's part?

That is what sets the scene for the rest of this book. It is important to note who or what is on trial: In actuality it is God who is on trial, and yet it was Job who thought he was the one who was on trial. Satan's accusation is blasphemous: '[God] has worshippers because he treats them well, but they are a loose bunch, for as soon as trouble comes, they fly the coop and forget about God!' That is what the best-case mortals can put up for their claim to love God. Yet everyone, just like the rest of mankind, will abandon God when trouble comes! Put in sermonic form, the question here is this: 'Will a Man or Woman Serve God for Nothing?' Do we serve God because He is an awesome and majestic God or do we serve Him because of all the blessings God has given us in the bargain? Do we mortals worship God because of what we can get out of it or because of our deep sense of gratitude for all He has done for us in our salvation and in our daily lives?

God accepts this diabolic challenge or wager of Satan's and replies in effect, 'Good and well, then. Let's test your theory. I have a man named Job who is blameless and upright. He fears me and he steers clear of evil.' (1:8). So Satan says in effect, 'Let me at him and you will see that I am correct!' Poor Job! He never volunteered to be God's parade example. I am sure if he had done so, and this same information about what was taking place in heaven had got to his ears, he would have volunteered a bunch of his other friends to take his place as much better examples than he. Who wants to be a trophy of suffering? That job would be just one big pain!

THE ETHICAL QUESTIONS RAISED BY JOB AND HIS BOOK

As Wheeler Robinson summarized the book of Job, 'Through all Job's thinking, the reality of God's *existence* remains unchallenged. The whole controversy is fought around [God's] alleged *character*.'[7] With that as the basis for all his thinking and speaking, Job was bothered instead by the question of what sort of God, who was so all-powerful, would still insist on His servant's suffering, but not for any personal or unconfessed sin?

But the issue of suffering could be stated in more than one way. Wheeler Robinson put it this way: 'How

---

7. H. Wheeler Robinson, *The Cross in the Old Testament*, (Philadelphia: Westminster Press, 1955), p. 23.

is it possible, in a world morally governed by a just and powerful God, for innocent men to suffer' as Job claimed he was suffering?[8] But that was not the only issue that was up for consideration. The prologue to the book poses quite a different question from Satan: 'Does Job fear God for nothing?' (1:9). Satan implies that humans are actually selfish and their love and professed piety before God is basically to get rewards from God. For Job's 'friends,' everything could be wrapped up in one tidy package: people suffer for their unconfessed sin. Your children sinned, so God paid them back for their sins (8:4). This is the idea of retributive justice. Thus the message of the three friends is this: sinners suffer, therefore avoid sin; however, on the other hand, the good prosper, therefore be good! Why is Job so blind to this solution, they wonder? Surely, this is the reason he is suffering!

At the height of Job's self-defense of his innocence, he mounts a monologue in chapters 29-31 that T. B. Maston correctly judged included 'some of the most exalted ethical material of the Old Testament.'[9] Job speaks of how in the past he had 'delivered the poor ... and the fatherless (29:13). Righteousness was his robe (14) and he was as eyes for the blind, feet to the lame, and a father to the poor and needy' (15, 16). But in chapter 31 Job makes his strongest defense, for as T. H. Robinson said: 'In chapter 31 we have the highest ethical standard which the Old Testament contains ... We never reach such a standard again until we

---

8. Ibid., p. 35.

9. T.B. Maston, 'Ethical Content of Job,' *Southwestern Journal of Theology,* 14 (1971): 51.

come to the teaching of Jesus Himself."[10] Robinson went on to assert:

> We have here a standard of moral conduct which is unequalled in the Old Testament, and comes nearer to the teaching of Jesus than anything else in the Bible.[11]

In chapter 31, Job takes up a number of hypothetical sinful deeds others think he may have committed, each of which he introduces with sixteen conditional 'If' clauses or sentences (31:5, 7, 9, 13, 16, 19, 20, 21, 24, 25, 26, 29, 31, 33, 38, and 39). By so doing, he clears himself of any sinful deed or even sinful intention. Elsewhere the Old Testament speaks of the inwardness of moral and ethical conduct, but here it is spelled out as clearly as we have ever seen it traced in biblical or philosophical writings. Job agrees with Jesus and the New Testament that it is out of the heart that the issues of life proceed.

Job in Earlier and more Recent Literature

In his recent book on Job, Rabbi Harold S. Kushner wrote:

> If there is more interest in the book of Job today among people who are not regular students of the Bible, I think we can attribute that to two things: to cancer and to Adolf Hitler.[12]

---

10. T. H. Robinson, *Job and His Friends*, (London: SCM Press, 1954), pp. 64-65.

11. Ibid., p. 111.

12. Harold S. Kushner, *The Book of Job: When Bad Things Happened to a Good Person.* Jewish Encounter Series, (New York: Nextbook, 2012), p. 165.

That may be partially true, but people have been suffering a good while before the appearance of either of these two situations. To take just one example. Recall that when the Lisbon earthquake hit in A.D. 1753, Voltaire wrote *Candide* as a response to his own question: How could a good God allow suffering like the Lisbon earthquake and on such a scale? Much later, Archibald MacLeish[13] wrote the play *J.B.* in an attempt to give some sense to the emptiness infesting most of twentieth-century life by arranging it around the life experiences of a modern Job. The Jewish writer Elie Wiesel[14] wrote the book *The Trial of God*, which somewhat mirrors the trial that Job attempted to bring against God as Wiesel dialogued about the Holocaust.

Even the philosopher Immanuel Kant[15] wrote a small book in 1791 entitled *On the Miscarriage of all Philosophical Trials in Theodicy.* Kant ended up challenging all attempts at explaining the existence of evil in this world that was created by God. The word 'Theodicy' was coined by the philosopher Gottfried Leibnitz as he argued that we live in the 'best of all possible worlds.' But Voltaire attacked such a concept in his *Candide* as he presented what he regarded as an improvement of the book of Job.

---

13. Archibald MacLeish, *J. B.: A Play in Verse,* (Boston: Houghton Mifflin, 1958).

14. Elie Wiesel, *The Trial of God (as it was held on February 25, 1649, in Shamgorod): A Play,* Translated by Marion Wiesel, (New York: Schocken, 1995).

15. Immanuel Kant, 'On the Miscarriage of All Philosophical Trials in Theodicy,' in *Religion and Rational Theology*, edited by Allen W. Wood and George di Giovanni, 21-37. Cambridge Edition of the Works of *Immanuel Kant,* (Cambridge University Press, 2001).

Wilhelm Vischer,[16] a Swiss Old Testament scholar, wrote his book on Job as things were building up to World War II. But because of his opposition to German National Socialism, he was exiled to Switzerland. Vischer argued that Job's conflict was not with desiring 'things,' but Job desired God's goodness, which he saw as being beyond good and evil.

Harold Kushner softened the book of Job as it stands and focused only on the poetry. Kushner saw three things as true in the book of Job: God must be all-powerful, God must be all good, but evil still exists. The solution to the problem of evil and the trial of Job lies hidden, according to Kushner, in God's second speech about the Behemoth and the Leviathan (Job 40–41). For Kushner, God designated two areas of creation[17] in which He would cede control: one was the domain of nature and natural law, the other was the area of 'human freedom to choose between good and evil.'[18]

TEACHING AND PREACHING FROM JOB

There is no doubt that Job speaks to some of the basic issues of our human experience. Yet, his book often is also one of the most neglected areas in current day teaching and preaching. The reasons for this neglect are as follows:

Job is a difficult book to teach and preach on, primarily because the speeches of Job's three visitors are not approved

---

16. Wilhelm Vischer, 'The Witness of Job to Jesus Christ,' *Evangelical Quarterly,* Vol. 48 (1934), 40-53; 138-50.

17. Kushner, p. 197.

18. Kushner, p. 198.

THE MAJESTY OF GOD IN THE MIDST OF INNOCENT SUFFERING

by the Lord (Job 42:7). In what sense, then, can these be used, if at all, as sources of divine revelation?

The book of Job seems to give a paucity of answers to the weighty problems of suffering and pain he raises. How then shall we describe its purpose in the Bible?

In order to teach and preach the book of Job, it requires additional time and preparation to sort out what is divinely taught and what is humanly offered. How can we mark this difference?

All too often suffering threatens and shakes the trust and faith of men and women, so some wrongly believe it is best to avoid it as a subject of the pulpit.

However, in spite of some of the obstacles, Job can pack a powerful message for our day. Here is the proposed outline for our study in this book.

Overview: Prologue

Job 1:	Facing the test of trials
Job 2:	Coping with the pressure of pain
Job 3–7:	Is it better to die than to live?
Job 8–11:	Reject foolish platitudes
Job 12–14:	We can plead our case
Job 15–19:	Help comes from on high
Job 20–26:	Will God ever intervene for me?
Job 27–31:	The folly of self-defense
Job 32–33:	Youth tries its hand at answering
Job 34–37:	Your God is too small
Job 38–40:5:	The God who created it all
Job 40:1–42:6:	The nature of God

The First Cycle

Chapter 1:
Job 1–2

Coping with the pressures
of pain

'Does Job fear God for nothing' (Job 1:9a).

1. GOD CHOOSES A MAN FROM THE EAST AS HIS MODEL SERVANT (1:1-5)

As we open up the book of Job, we are given our first glimpse of the burning question that has bothered all of us at one time or another: 'Why do we mortals suffer if God is so good and so powerful?' But rather than beginning philosophically, or even theologically, we are treated to a biographical sketch of a man whose name was 'Job.' We are told that he had four distinctive qualities: he (1) 'feared God', (2) he 'steered clear of evil,' and he was (3) 'blameless' and (4) 'upright,' or 'straight,' in the sense that he did not deviate from God's standards or ways (1:1). This is no ordinary man; he is truly an unusual person, who is without moral blemish, yet he also is a man who chooses to reject and avoid all forms of evil. Instead, he submits to God's person and teachings. That estimate is not just a human or a boastful self-assessment:

God Himself repeats that description of Job in 1:8 and in 2:3. So, this estimate of the man Job is altogether true!

But just as quickly we are told about how wealthy Job is, for in 1:2-3 we are given an account of how blessed this man of God is. He had seven sons, three daughters, 7,000 sheep, 3,000 camels, 500 yoke of oxen, 500 donkeys, and a large retinue of servants, not to mention his possible impressive holdings in land. He is indeed 'the greatest man among all the people of the east' (1:3c). Scripture identifies the 'men of the east' as being from the same place as 'Kedar,' which was in the northern portion of Arabia (Jer. 49:28). So this is the man God chose as His candidate to vindicate the position the Lord had taken in His wager with Satan. Job was both godly and wealthy. But Job evidenced two characteristics that do not often go together: he was both godly and wealthy! How could it have happened that a mere mortal could both revere God and be fabulously wealthy at one and the same time? Does this text indeed imply that it is really possible for a man to be godly and yet at the same time also to be wealthy? Had not all these gifts Job possessed come from his Heavenly Father? But is it not also true that possessions, more often than not, turn our hearts away from God if they become the object of our affections? Yet in Job's case he did not choose to be wrongly influenced by all the wealth he had, for he loved and feared God and took a broad circle away from all evil. No wonder this is a story worthy of being told! It is a refreshingly new perspective on the matter of walking with God and yet not letting the gifts and possessions God has given to mortals turn their heads and hearts away from Him.

We are given a further glimpse of Job's godly character in the concern he expressed for his grown children. Every year each of his seven sons would give a birthday party on each one of the sons' birthdays (called a 'feast,' or 'his day,' 1:4). Yet, ever vigilant for his children's spirituality, Job would offer a burnt offering for the forgiveness of his children's sins, lest they had sinned, or even secretly cursed God in their hearts (1:5). This is how Job acted routinely! (1:5d).

2. God allows Satan to test Job's family and possessions to prove his point (1:6-22)

But things are about to change suddenly in life as Job knows it, for in 1:6 there came a day when 'the sons of God' (a.k.a. the 'angels') presented themselves (Hebrew, literally 'stationed themselves') before God to report on what they had been doing. Satan also reports on his activities along with the angelic reports. Satan's report includes a global patrol, apparently in keeping with what 1 Peter 5:8 disclosed as a general principle: Satan had been going back and forth throughout the whole earth looking for those he could accuse or devour. Satan must have given at that meeting an adverse report on some of God's inconsistent saints. God must have countered Satan's accusations, for suddenly the Lord brings up the name of His servant Job and gives him very high marks for consistent obedience by saying: 'There is no one on earth like him; he is a blameless and upright, a man who fears God and shuns evil' (1:8b). To have such praise come from God about a mortal is high praise indeed!

Satan refuses to buy such high accolades for a mere mortal, for instead of getting into an argument with God about Job or any of the characteristics already noted, Satan chooses to attack Job's motives for his godliness. He questions just why it is that Job is so righteous. He thinks he knows, for it is all a put-up-job; Job serves God so faithfully simply because of all that he gets out of it! (1:9). God has been good to Job. So Satan challenges God to remove the hedge with which He had surrounded and protected Job, his possessions, and his household, and he announces that Job will surely curse God to His face in that eventuality (1:11b). Anyone who serves God only does so, mocks Satan, for what they can get out of it. According to the devil, worship, is a selfish deal. If God removes His protecting hand from any of His people, then you will see their true colors begin to show, claimed Satan in effect. If the Church does not produce some economic or social advantages for being a member, this accuser of the brethren, Satan, will continue to rant and rave in his accusations against them and God. But when trouble comes, he bragged, then the crowds will begin to drift away. Perhaps this is why many radio and television preachers have decided to promote a health, wealth, and prosperity gospel message, much as Tetzel had promised when he was raising funds to build St Peter's cathedral in Rome during the days of the Reformation. Alternatively, this has led others, as Bonhoeffer had likewise warned in his *Cost of Discipleship*, to adopt a 'cheap grace' in lieu of a 'costly grace' approach to the worship of the Lord. This is a salvation and Christian life that makes no demands of total commitment on our present lives for the gift of eternal life in the future. But that too is a bogus offer! God works in altogether different ways. Our Lord knows the difference between mere 'show' and true reality!

To show that Satan is wrong, the Lord agrees to let Satan use Job as a test case for his bold thesis that mortals only serve God for what they can get out of it (1:12-22). Therefore, God permits Satan to attack all of Job's possessions. Later, a second test would attack Job's health as well (2:1-10). Satan leaves the heavenly presence of the Lord and goes off to prepare his assault on brother Job (1:12b). Hard times were ahead of Job!

The devilish assaults come one day with one right after the other, always with only one servant spared from the effects of the tragedy, so he could bring the bad news to Job (1:15b, 16b, 17c, 19c). The evil one used human sources as well as natural forces to do his work and to make sure Job got the point. First, the people called the Sabeans (who seemed to hail from the region of Sheba in southwest Arabia, or alternatively from Sheba[1] near Dedan in Upper Arabia), stole 1,000 oxen and 500 donkeys (1:15). Then the 'fire of God,' perhaps a series of lightning-bolt strikes, took out 7,000 sheep all at once (1:16). Then the Chaldeans attacked out of the north and stole 3,000 camels, coming

---

1. Some factors such as the age of Job seem to suggest Job was written in the patriarchal age. There are at least three references which point to a much more recent age, no earlier than 1000 B.C. The first of these is the reference to Sheba. See Edwin M. Yamauchi, *Africa and the Bible*, (Baker Academic, Grand Rapids, Michigan, 2009), pp. 90-97. The second reason is the reference to the Chaldeans. See Edward M. Blaiklock, *The New International Dictionary of Biblical Archaeology*, (Regency Reference Library/Zondervan Publishing House, Grand Rapids, Michigan), 1983, pp. 123-125. The third reason is discussed on page 140.

at Job's servants in three companies, perhaps attacking from all three sides at the same time (1:17). Finally, the *coup d'etat* against Job came, as what many would regard as the last straw, for a tornado windstorm struck the building where Job's seven sons and three daughters were celebrating a birthday, so that the house fell in on them and they all were lost (1:18-19). Job now is without any of his livestock, any of his transportation, any of his servants, or any of his children; all he has are the four messengers who had been spared to make sure the bad news got back to Job, coming one right after the other to him. Suddenly Job plummets in one fell swoop from being one of the richest men of the area to being a pauper sitting on an ash-heap. Now what will he do? Will he prove the devil correct and curse God? Or will he still keep on trusting God?

In response to so savage an assault on all his property and family, Job tears his robe in deep grief and shaves his head (1:20). He falls to the ground, but not in despair, but in worship and obeisance to God. With that he utters these remarkable words:

> Naked I came from my mother's womb, and naked I will depart. The LORD gave and the LORD has taken away; may the name of the LORD be praised. (1:21).

Job must have felt just as he did the day he came out of his mother's womb. Even though he was not naked literally, he certainly felt he had been stripped of all that he had owned. Under the impact of such an enormous amount of horrible news, Job recognized God's sovereign rights to all he was and to all he had previously owned. How many of us would have reacted in such a manner?

But Job retained his moral integrity and refused to give in to bitterness or to offer recriminations against God or others. He held his tongue and his faith remained intact. Satan had lost his wager with God, and he had lost dramatically, to say the least. Job was not at all one of the selfish or one of the fickle creatures Satan had depicted all mortals to be. But Satan did not give up easily; he still had another plan of attack.

3. God allows Satan to attack his servant's body (2:1-10)

The evil one is indeed the accuser of the brethren, for once again the scene turns towards heaven as it is time for another heavenly angelic consultation (2:1). Apparently as usual, Satan shows up for the celestial meeting as he gives the same report: he has been traversing the globe as usual in his diabolical business (2:2). Yahweh quizzed Satan by asking him in effect, 'What do you think of my servant Job now?' (2:3). 'Isn't he just as I said he was: Blameless, upright, one who feared me and who shunned evil?' (2:3b).

Satan's retort is cynical and cruel: 'Skin for skin,' that's what I say, claims this bold accuser of the brethren. Job was willing to suffer the loss of his kids' skins, Satan may have reasoned, but I tell you Job will think differently when it comes to his own body; then he will curse you to your face just as I have predicted! (2:4). That will be the last straw. He will worship you as his God as long as you don't touch his body. But if you stretch out your hand and strike his flesh, skin or his bones, I tell you he will curse you to your face, remonstrates the devil (2:5).

31

Once again the wager is on, for God now gives Satan permission to touch Job's body, but God demands that Job's life must be spared; Satan cannot kill Job (2:6), for that belongs to God. Now Job's health is on the line this time instead of his possessions – as they had been in the first test. As a result, Job immediately is afflicted with sores and painful boils from the crown of his head to the soles of his feet (2:7). The word 'sore/painful boils' is the same word used of one of the ten plagues of Egypt (Exod. 9:8-11; Deut. 28:27), and the word used of Hezekiah's illness (2 Kings 20:7). We are unable to say just what disease it was that Satan threw at him, whether it was smallpox, elephantiasis, chronic eczema, psoriasis, leprosy[2], or some other grave illness. But Job did tell us some of his symptoms: those sores were inflamed, ulcerous (2:7), itching (2:8), and producing degenerative changes in his facial skin (2:7, 12). Job lost his appetite (3:24); he faced depression (3:24-25), and worms lunched on the boils (7:5), with pustular sores and hardened skin (7:5) as he experienced difficulty breathing (9:18), as well as having bad breath (19:17), dark eyelids (16:16), loss of weight (19:20; 33:21), continual pain (30:17), blackened skin (30:30) and fever (30:30). This must have been going on for some time before his three visitors came to 'comfort' him. (7:3; 29:2).

Job left his home and went to sit on 'the ashes' in the ash-heap or dump just outside the city. To relieve his

---

2. Leprosy (Hansen's Disease) is not attested for the OT period. 'Leprosy' is a mistranslation in English Versions. See 'Diseases & Plagues,' *Dictionary of Daily Life in Biblical and Post-Biblical Antiquity* [DDL], (Hendrickson Publishers, Massachusetts, 2016). For the significance of ashes, see 'Mourning & Weeping,' DDL.

itching and the build-up of pus, he took a piece of broken pottery and began scraping his skin (2:8) on the city dump in the place where beggars and outcasts of society hung out with the wild dogs. Perhaps he used the ashes as a sort of talcum powder to sooth the itching from his boils. How demeaning and humiliating for one who had once sat at the village gate as an elder and local judge (29:7) to now find himself in such lowly circumstances – sitting on the ash-heap of the city-dump!

But the final straw seemed to come when his wife confronted him with this question: 'Are you [still] maintaining your integrity?' (2:9). '[Why don't you just] curse God and die!' (2:9b). She too had also become a tool of Satan in his attack on Job, for when she urged Job to curse God, that is exactly what the devil had declared Job would do (1:11; 2:5). What a blow? Just when we expect and need sympathy and words of comfort, we are sometimes attacked further by those who love us most.

The Jewish Targum of Job called his wife by the name of 'Dinah,' but the apocryphal work of the Testament of Job, which possibly comes from the pre-Christian era, called her 'Sitis.' This Greek apocryphal work came from the pre-Christian era, for it seems to have many verbal similarities to the Septuagint (Greek) version of Job. The Testament of Job went on to place quite an extensive speech in her mouth. She is alleged to have also said:

> For how long will you exercise patience, saying, 'See, I will persevere a little longer, waiting and hoping for my redemption?' For consider, the memory of you has vanished from the earth, your sons and your daughters

are no more – those who were the pains and travail of my womb, for whom I exhausted myself in vain. As for you, there you sit, your body rotting amid worms, and spending the nights in the open air. While I, wandering about a slave, roaming restlessly hither and thither, from house to house, await the hour of sunset that I may rest from my weariness and from my sorrows which now press upon me. Curse God and die!

The Testament of Job tells quite a story about Job. For example, in a farewell address to his seven sons and three daughters, all of whom are given names not found in the Bible, Job informs them that he is of the generation of Abraham, a descendant of Esau and was called at first 'Jobab' before God called him 'Job'. Job's second wife, the mother of this new generation of ten children, was Jacob's daughter Dinah. Job, like Abraham, had switched loyalties from pagan idols to the worship of the true God. Therefore, Job destroyed the idols in the land and was told that for doing so he should prepare for a lifelong battle with Satan. However, there seems to be no way presently to confirm such a story!

4. God allows three of Job's friends to further test him (2:11-13)

The book of Job calls these three visitors Job's 'friends' (2:11), but that designation will not be any more accurate than calling them Job's 'comforters.' (16:2). Somehow these three heard of all the trouble/evil that had befallen Job. Tragic news tends to travel much faster than good news for some reason. So they decided to visit their 'friend.'

The three men were no doubt also themselves wealthy sheiks like Job who had come quite some distance to be of what help they could to their 'friend' Job. Never do they share how they learned about Job's recent losses, or how they gained the theology they shared, but when they saw Job, apparently they had no idea of the depth of Job's anguish and afflictions. They seem to have had no trouble, however, communicating with each other or Job, so they seemed to have spoken the same language and to have shared many of the same observations and illustrations on life which a believer like Job possessed, for they clearly understood each other very well.

The three men apparently had agreed to meet at the same time, so they could travel and arrive together. They each came from their own place (2:11) in order to sympathize with Job. But when they saw Job, Job was so disfigured from the disease that had afflicted him that they hardly recognized him. So impacted were they by what they saw that they expressed their grief in four ways: (1) they wailed, because of their emotional shock, (2) they openly wept in sorrow over what had happened to Job, (3) they tore their robes in broken-heartedness in a typical near eastern demonstration of grief, and (4) they threw dust over their heads as a sign that they were completely helpless to restore Job to his previous state of health (2:12).

Eliphaz is an Edomite name and he came from Teman. Gen. 36:4 records that a son born to Esau and Adah also was named Eliphaz. Moreover, there was a city named 'Teman' in both Edom and a 'Tema' in Arabia, where its citizens were known for their 'wisdom' (Jer. 49:7; Obad. 8). Bildad came from 'Shuah,' but this name is unattested elsewhere in the Bible even though the name 'Shuah' does occur as a son of Abraham by his concubine Keturah (Gen. 25:2; 1 Chron. 1:32). Zophar came from 'Naamath,' a name that etymologically means 'beautiful,' but it too appears nowhere else in the Old Testament. Some think the town mentioned here was a Judean town (Josh. 15:41), but that does not seem at all likely. Finally, a fourth, but younger, friend appears much later in the book of Job named Elihu (Job 32).

The three older men sit on the ground in silence with Job for 'seven days and seven nights' (2:13). Even though they offered no words of sympathy, one can imagine possible groans of anguish and grief as they just sat and tried to get their minds around what had happened to Job. Of course, their silence could well have been as a result of the fact that they were horrified at what had overtaken Job. This was awful.

However, we the readers have been tipped off ahead of time in the prologue that Job was not the cause of his suffering. We know something the 'friends' did not know – that Satan was the instigator of Job's troubles. One of the key reasons why this suffering was being permitted by God was to answer the Satanic question: 'Will men and women serve God gratis?' 'If nothing is to be gained from worshipping God and serving him, will mortals still serve God anyway?' Job's friends, however, got it all wrong. For if Job was an innocent sufferer, then such suffering could happen to them as well. Their view of God was too small to allow such innocent suffering to ever take place; there had to be sin in one's life, or some awesome things awaited them up ahead in life as well!

Conclusions

1. Job's troubles began because God selected him as an example of one who loved Him and served Him for his own sake and not for what he got out of it. This should correct some poor health, wealth, and prosperity preaching and teaching around the world today!

2. Job's three friends come from the same neighboring areas where some of the descendants of Esau came from.

3. Job was stripped of all his possessions and then he was stripped of his health. He was one broken man!

4. Job's wife did not seem a noble character, for whether out of sympathy or just plain tiredness, she recommended that Job take the course of action that Satan was betting on: 'Curse God!'

5. In the end, Job's three friends may have, under God, provided more of the heat of his affliction than the sores themselves gave.

QUESTIONS FOR REFLECTION
AND DISCUSSION

1. What four characteristics did God attribute to Job's character as He spoke with Satan?

2. Did this mean Job was without any sin? Can any mortal be totally without any sin in this world today?

3. Why do you think that Job prayed that his children might be forgiven if they had cursed God in their hearts? What does this teach us about intercessory prayer for others?

4. Why do you think that birthdays were good occasions for a family feast? Why is it that Job and his wife were not invited to such festivities?

5. How is it that Satan is invited to a heavenly consultation? How could heaven be pure with Satan there? What does Satan's accusation of Job tell us about his characteristics?

6. Did Job vindicate God's claims about him and did Job falter in the bet that he would curse God?

Chapter 2:
Job 3:1–5:27

Job longing for death and Eliphaz's chastening of him

'Is it not better to die than live?'

Job 3:1-26 and Jeremiah 20:14-18 are two rivals for a possible award for being the most depressing chapters in the whole Bible. Therefore, few sermons select either of these chapters as the basis for an exposition in Church on the Lord's day; instead, they are viewed as chapters that depict the lowest point in the emotional experiences and lives of both Job and the prophet Jeremiah. As such, then, they attract very little attention from the pulpit. But for those who find themselves in the midst of suffering, they give voice to many a hurting heart!

The first two words in Job 3:1, 'After this,' are no doubt a reference to the series of losses and tragedies that Job has just experienced in the previous two chapters. But then we are told that Job 'opened his mouth and cursed his day' (3:1, my literal translation for 'the day [of his birth]'). We should not suppose that by 'his day' Job was referring to his destiny or his future; instead, he clearly refers to the 'day ... [on] which [he] was born' (3), thus the paraphrase in most of our English Bibles is correct. But it is also clear that with an outburst of anguish, Job regrets that he had ever been born (3:1-10), for he wishes that he indeed had been born dead (3:11-19); or if not, he now states how he longs to die (3:20-26). It would appear that those seven days of silence from his three 'friends' had sharpened his sense of loss and caused him to reflect on the unfairness and complete injustice of what had happened to him as if it became clear to him all of a sudden. How was he to account for such a batch of trouble? If God is good all the time, and all the time God is good, then, what on earth had gone wrong?

1. JOB WISHES HE HAD NOT BEEN BORN (3:1-10)

Job begins to vent his anguish by wishing he had never been born and that even that day might have been wiped clean off the calendar. In fact, he even wished that the night he had been conceived would have been erased as well, even prior to the event of his birth some nine months later (3:3b). It is worthwhile noting that Job and the Scriptures here point to the fact that the beginning of one's existence, i.e. the beginning of life, commences with conception rather than as some modern theories place it, at the time when a mother first feels movement in her womb in the fifth month, or even later according to some, at the time of birth. Even the 'night' in which he was conceived, is personified as if the night itself knew and announced that a male child had been conceived on that very night! Thus, the night Job was 'conceived' was regarded as the time when he first began to exist, or live, contrary to modern so-called scientific-claims. So disheartened was Job that he charged that 'night' with an injustice in letting him be born. Poor Job – he was at one of his lowest points of despondency.

Job goes on to give more details on the day of his birth (4-5) and to enlarge on what he thinks about the night of his conception (6-9). Verse 4 has two 'Let nots:' 'let not God (Hebrew, *Eloah*) above care for it,' and '[Let not] light shine on it [that night!]' Verse 10 concludes this poetic unit by supplying us with the reason why Job longed for the removal of his birthday from the calendar.

In a dramatic reversal of God introducing 'light' in Genesis 1:3, Job despondently prays, 'May that day [of my birth] be darkness' (3:4). I suppose he wanted it to be dark so he could slip by being born without any notice by anyone or by God. Job refers to 'darkness,' five times, and here he uses four different Hebrew words for 'darkness.' For example, in 3:5, he asks for 'darkness' and 'black gloom' (3:5). The Hebrew word for 'darkness,' this time in 3:5c, is used only in this verse in Job, but it does not appear in the rest of the Old Testament. It refers to the 'blackness' of an eclipse, a tornado, or an intense storm. Job even hopes that God would wipe the night of his conception off the calendar so it would not be counted in the actual number of days and nights (3:6b-c).

Job goes on to pray that the night of his conception (3:7) might 'be barren,' in which he uses the word that literally means 'stony' – i.e. apparently, that either his mother or his father might be as unproductive as 'stony' ground! And whereas people in the Near East shouted for joy when a baby was born, Job says in 3:7, 'Let no joyful shout enter (Hebrew literally, 'pierce') it [the night].'

Job even raises the specter of 'rousing Leviathan' (3:8b) to curse the day of his birth. The 'Leviathan' appears in Canaanite literature of Ugarit and Phoenicia as a sea monster, who on the occasion of an eclipse is said to swallow up the sun or the moon. This does not mean that Job believed in the mythology of Canaan; instead, it may merely have meant that he was appropriating the images that were known in his day and age for his own poetic literary purposes. Accordingly, if one of the luminaries in the heavens suddenly disappeared, then there might also be hope, as Job saw it, in his mixed up mental state of despondency, i.e., that his birthday might also be missing in a manner similar to disappearing luminaries in the heavens. Thus, he wished the 'morning stars' (usually said to be the planets of Venus and Mercury) would be darkened so that they too would give no light on the night he was conceived. The opening of the 'doors of the womb' that bore Job is another way to depict his conception, not his birth. If his mother's womb did not open, then Job would not have been conceived (3:10) and 'trouble' would have been hidden from his eyes (3:10b). Job needs comfort and help, for he is grief-stricken to the nth-degree.

2. JOB WISHES HE HAD DIED AT BIRTH (3:11-19)

Since Job's wish that the night of his conception and the day of his birth would have been blotted off the calendar has not been granted, he proceeds to wish that he had at least been stillborn (3:11). Cursing the night of his conception and his birthday were not enough for the release of pain and suffering he had faced. Why, then, was he not at least born dead? A miscarriage, or a stillbirth, would then have been his second choice rather than receiving life (3:11-12). To give prominence to his wishes, Job asks two questions: Why didn't I die at birth? And why didn't the knees that received me and the breasts that nursed me give out? The reference to knees that received him seems to refer to the custom of placing the newborn child on the father's knees (Gen. 48:12), a symbol the child was his own.

Job was in one sad state of mind, for he goes on in 3:13-15 to describe how much better it would have been had he died at birth, for then he would have known peace and rest from his upcoming troubles! And if death did not come at birth, then why did it not come when he was a child? Had he been given rest in death as a child, he could have rested with the notable kings, and the rich princes (3:14-15), who already were resting in their graves. Job depicts death as a 'restful' condition in the earth. He plaintively asks: Why was my fetus not hidden, or buried in the ground (3:16)? At least in that place in the grave he would 'cease from turmoil' and be 'at rest' (3:17). In that place Job would no longer suffer disease, or be a slave to the shout of the slave-driver (3:17-18). In death he would be with the small and the great (3:19). Job's pleas for a divine release from his suffering are put in one phrase after another as he reflects not only on his own suffering, but that of so many others who likewise face grief and pain in the extreme.

3. Job again wishes that he would die (3:20-26)

Now for the third time Job asks 'Why?' (3:20, 11, 12). Once more he returns to the subject of light and darkness to depict life and death. His question in this section of verses 20-26 is best summarized in 3:21, Why is it that those who long for death, do not find it, even though they search and dig for it more than those who go digging for hidden treasure? When those who suffer finally 'find the grave,' they 'rejoice greatly' (3:22).

Then for the fourth time, Job once more uses the interrogative 'Why?' in chapter 3 (3:23) – 'Why am I Job so bewildered by God's work of hedging me in?' Such suffering deprived Job, he thought, of any hope in what was to come and restricted his movement from what he had known prior to this. Now for the first time, Job declares that it was God who had brought his sufferings and afflictions on him. Why, even Job's food made him groan at the very sight of it, meaning I guess that he had lost all his appetite, and his food did not please him, but repulsed him (3:24).

What Job had feared might happen to him had now taken place (3:25), for when he heard of one loss, he feared another loss would follow. Job summarizes his condition in 3:26. He could find no quietness, no rest, but only turmoil (3:26). Job was not finished with his questions by a long shot, for he posed at least ten questions throughout his long discourse with his three 'comforters' (3:11, 12, 20, 23; 7:20, 21; 9:29; 13:24; 21:4; 24:1). Each will be seen in our journey through the book of Job!

But on top of all of this, Job is next to be assailed by three men who claim to be his friends, but who turn out to be an even more bitter pill to swallow.

4. Job is rebuked by his 'friend' Eliphaz (4:1–5:18)

Job is visited by three of his companions: Eliphaz, Bildad, and Zophar. Their intentions and motives are honest and pure (at least at first) as they sit with their friend Job for a week-long time of silence, out of respect for all he has suffered. But when Job breaks the silence and begins to speak, they are shocked and startled by Job's claim that he is innocent and unfairly picked on by God. To cite just a few times where Job continues to make this point, let us recall the following:

- The arrows of the Almighty are in me (6:4).
- Although I am blameless … He [God] mocks the despair of the innocent' (9:21a, 23b).
- You [Lord] have put my feet in shackles; you keep close watch on all my paths (13:27).
- All was well with me, but he [God] shattered me … and crushed me (16:12).
- He [God] counts me among his enemies (19:11b).

Job feels that he has been unfairly singled out by God for rebuke and punishment, even though he does not deserve it. In six of his eight speeches he longs to personally present his case before God Himself (9:3; 13:3; 16:21; 19:23; 23:4; 31:35). Then he could show God how what was happening to him was unfair and uncalled for!

But Job's three friends are just as adamant that Job is an obvious sinner, one who just needs to repent, for if he did, then he would receive relief from all his distress. Their reasoning goes along the lines of this syllogism:

- Major Premise: All suffering is the result of punishment for sin;
- Minor: Job is suffering;
- Conclusion: Therefore, Job is a sinner who must confess his sin and repent before God!

It is for this reason that what a man gets in life is dependent on what he has done. On this point, the three 'comforters' remain unshakeable and they become increasingly vitriolic. At first, in the first round of their speeches (in chapters 4-14), the three men gently hint at the real presence of Job's sin, but in round two they move from mere suggestion that sin is the problem to an open insinuation that this is indeed Job's problem. However, by the time we come to the third round of speeches (in chapters 21-27), the accusations are out in the open and often brutal.

A. Eliphaz rebukes Job based on his experience (4:1-6)

Three times over Eliphaz repeats in his speeches the words: 'I have seen' (4:8; 5:3; 15:17). Eliphaz is more courteous to Job than Bildad and not at all as blunt and as accusatory of Job as Zophar, yet nevertheless, Eliphaz too presumes Job is guilty of some sin that needs to be confessed right away.

So the first to respond to Job's jeremiad was Eliphaz, who no doubt was the oldest of the three 'friends.' As Job sits on the ash-heap, Eliphaz begins with a rebuke in which he fears Job might impetuously and impatiently not listen to what he had to say (4:2). This 'friend' did graciously recall how Job had previously instructed so many others who had stumbled, yet which neighbors had nevertheless been strengthened and supported during the days of their troubles (4:3-4). But now that the shoe was on the other foot, when trouble had come knocking at Job's door, the questions were these: Should Job not be just as patient as he had advised others to be in the past? (4:5-6). Where, asks Job's interrogator, should your piety and hope be in your time of trouble? (4:6).

B. Eliphaz gives his theory about suffering (4:7-11)
In the thinking of this 'comforter,' innocent persons just do not suffer, neither do the upright experience destruction; rather, it is only the person who plows iniquity and sows trouble that will harvest trouble and reap the anger of God (4:7-9). According to Eliphaz, bad guys always lose, but good guys always win.

Job thinks that his former strength has been shattered and scattered by the loss of his children, just like the voice of the hungry lion and its teeth have been broken so that these lionesses and their cubs die for lack of prey to eat (4:10-11). But is Job as helpless as all of this? Is this the right picture of a man who feared God and steered away from evil?

C. Eliphaz describes a vision he had had (4:12-21)
Eliphaz relates how his bones shook (14) and his hair stood on end (15) one night as he began to fall into a deep sleep. Eliphaz had an experience of a spirit 'glid[ing] past [his] face' (15a), it stopped, remained quiet, then spoke in a whisper the following words:

> Can a [weak] mortal (Hebrew, `enosh) be more righteous
> than God?
> Can even a strong man (Hebrew, *gaber*) be more pure
> than his Maker? (4:17)

These words (and the rest of the whispered words in verses 18-21 are the words Eliphaz claims he has heard in his dream, but he does not assert that these were words of revelation that came from God, for he claims these words came to him 'secretly' or 'stealthily' (4:12,) and not directly from Yahweh. He meant to imply that such could not be the case; weak, fallible mortals cannot rival the righteousness of God, nor can even so-called valiant strong men exceed the purity of their Maker. The saying of course contains truth, but Eliphaz was way off base to apply this saying to Job. So, there was a good mark for Eliphaz's teaching, but it carried a bad notation for the application Eliphaz made when he applied it to Job! Job was not experiencing distress and suffering because he was either weak as a mortal, or because he was impure before God. Job was not being paid back for what he deserved! We, the readers, know this already from the introduction and for the Lord's remarkable characterization of Job.

Eliphaz waxes eloquent on man's mortality in verses 18-23. If God did not trust His angels, but charged even them with error, then why should our Lord be even more willing to charge mortal humans who are living in bodies made out of ordinary clay and dust? (18-19a). Men and women can be crushed like someone smashes a moth, or lets a vessel fall to the ground (19b, 20a). Why, the death of mortal humans was as easily accomplished as pulling up the cords tied to the tent pegs so that the whole tent collapses – just so a person suddenly dies without wisdom (21).

D. Eliphaz's recommendation to Job (5:1-27)

Eliphaz taunts Job with the suggestion that he could call on the angels to intervene on his behalf, but such a call would be useless (5:1) because angels cannot be trusted (4:18). Furthermore, Eliphaz thinks that the 'resentment' Job had displayed in his lament in chapter 3 was foolish, for such outbursts would end up killing Job (5:2-3). Even more heartless was the fact that Eliphaz brought up Job's loss of his children and his loss of his possessions (5:4-5). His point was going to be that calamities do not come from the external happenings to mortals; instead they come from within mortals, which trouble is as endemic to mortals as sparks fly up from a fire (5:7). So trouble comes to men and women from men and women themselves. But Eliphaz's view is too shortsighted, for remember Jesus' statement in the New Testament about the tower that fell on people (Luke 13:4). Jesus asked: 'Were they more wicked than the others who did not suffer that calamity? He answered, "No, they were not!"'

So, based on Eliphaz's view that all suffering is the result of personal sin, which needs to be recompensed, he recommends that if he were in Job's place, he would seek God and place his cause before the Lord (5:8). But Eliphaz was not suffering at that point, so why should he say or imply, 'If I were you, Job'? The point was this: he wasn't Job! Eliphaz goes on to make points that were nevertheless true, but unfortunately they did not fit Job's case. For instance, he taught that God was One who performed miracles that went way beyond any mortal's ability to fathom them (5:9); moreover, had not our Lord graciously sent rain that watered the countryside (5:10)? Had not God lifted up those who mourned and were downcast (5:11)? And had he not thwarted the plans for those who thought they were so skilled (5:12-14), as well as he rescued the needy, the poor, and those caught in the clutches of the powerholders of that day (5:15-16)? Furthermore, Eliphaz added a true saying, but one that once again was wrongly aimed at Job, that when God corrects a person, they should not despise the discipline of the Lord. Thus, Eliphaz taught good theology, but he incorrectly applied it to Job for he thought that God was disciplining Job for some evil he had done, which was incorrect (5:17). It is possible to teach what is true and accurate, but simultaneously to make the wrong application to the wrong person.

Accordingly, Job's 'friend' begged him to acknowledge his guilt, for then God would bless him. Job would receive God's rescue (5:19), his deliverance from famine (5:20), war (5:20b), slander (5:21), and from the wild animals (5:22b). If Job would only confess his sin, then his home would once again be secure, nothing would be missing on his property, his children would be numerous, and he would go to the grave full of vigor and full of days, just as the sheaves of grain were stacked up at harvest time, he too would also have lived a full term of life to produce the food from his fields ((5:26; cf. 42:17).

Eliphaz concludes, in an arrogant way, by reminding Job that all that he had said was based on his own investigations, so it would be best if Job heeded what had been said (5:27). Poor Job; he needed comfort but got rebuke instead! Surely God was simultaneously aware of all that was going on, but waited for the work He wanted accomplished in Job to be concluded first.

Conclusions

1. The conversation that took place on a garbage dump of ashes, apparently outside the town where Job lived, with Job's three friends, was one where his interlocutors missed by miles what ailed Job.

2. Job, on the other hand, was not a paragon of virtue, for he despaired so badly of living with his afflictions that he wanted the day of his conception and birth removed from the calendar of the world.

3. We can understand why he asked 'Why?' so frequently, but even though he feared God and took a wide path around evil, yet his humanity and pride still were showing through his complaints as he urged God to meet him so he could make his case before the Almighty.

4. However, Job never denied or cursed God as Satan had bet he would when he was deprived of all his possessions, children, and his health. In that sense Job was still strong!

5. Eliphaz based too much of his speech on experience and not enough on solid teaching from God above and His word of revelation. Moreover, he was poor at applying the truths he did speak, for they were altogether inappropriately applied to Job.

6. Eliphaz's view of the reason or purpose of suffering was too narrow (retributive suffering) and therefore he failed to connect with Job.

QUESTIONS FOR REFLECTION
AND DISCUSSION

1. Who won the bet Satan made with the Lord about Job and why? Satan or God?

2. What was wrong with Eliphaz's view of the cause and purpose of suffering in a believer's life?

3. Can you name from chapters 4 and 5 some of the true teachings that Eliphaz taught? But if it was true teaching, why did God say the opposite in Job 42:7?

4. Why does God send blessings on His mortals who believe in Him? Did Eliphaz teach what was proper in this regard? What then was the problem with his teaching?

5. Can you formulate a better view than Eliphaz's view for the teaching of the purpose and reason for suffering in the life of a believer?

Chapter 3:
Job 6:1–10:22

Job defends his complaining and lectures Bildad on God's greatness

(Job 6:1–10:22)

The first reply of Job to the speeches from the first of his 'comforters' named Eliphaz, came in Job 6:1–7:21 and consists of the following six parts:

- Job defends his complaining – 6:1-7
- Job despairs of finding relief from his suffering – 6:8-13
- Job expresses his disappointment in his friends – 6:14-23
- Job makes a plea to his three 'comforters'/counselors – 6:24-30
- Job describes his misery – 7:1-6
- Job prays to God – 7:7-21

1. ANSWERS TO ELIPHAZ – THE SUBJECTIVIST AND ELDER DREAMER (6:1-7)

A. Job defends his complaining first of all (6:1-7)
Job had mentioned in 5:19 'From six calamities he will rescue [me], in seven no harm will touch [me].' With that teaching as his assurance, Job at first makes no attempt

to respond directly to Eliphaz, who apparently was the oldest of the three men; instead he launches into another complaint about his condition. Moreover, even when he does finally get around to responding to Eliphaz, he addresses all three men together ('Your, you' in 6:25-30; 7:12-21 use plural pronouns), instead of directing his remarks only to Eliphaz.

Job must have felt that some sort of explanation was needed, for he had uttered what most would have regarded as rash and impetuous words in chapter 3. Therefore, he moans in effect, 'Why shouldn't I complain?' He is so loaded down with the weight of his suffering that he claims it easily outweighed the sand of the sea (6:3), when all his pain had been put on a scale (2). Job accuses God of shooting arrows of poison into him (4). What is more, he judges that the weight of his problems exceeds anything one could expect – especially from God! How can he hold together at one and the same time the concept that the God he has known in previous days and the God he now thinks is attacking him are one and the same? If a donkey did not bray, or an ox low, when both were well fed, then neither would Job have complained if God had not marshaled such terrors against him (4b-5). Just as tasteless food needs salt if it is to have any flavor, in the same way they shouldn't be surprised if along with Job's troubles comes his complaining as well, for these two go together, just like salt and tasteless food go together (6-7).

B. Job despairs of finding relief from his suffering (6:8-13)
Since in Job's theology, God is sovereign over all, Job rightly identifies God as the source of all his grief and

pain. But Job also knows that God is at the same time the sustainer of all life. When Job puts both of these truths together, his 'request' is that God would be willing to take his hand from His act of sustaining his life and that God would 'crush' him as He 'cut off his life' (8-9). Job is begging God to let him die, for if he was going to die, this would result in two immediate benefits: he could endure his pain knowing that death would come soon (10b,) and secondly, he would not have 'denied the words of the Holy One' (10c).

In the meantime, what could Job depend on to keep him going (11)? What did Job's friends think? Did they assume he had the strength of a stone to hold up under the duress and the weight of his suffering (12a)? Or did they think he had flesh made out of 'bronze' (12)? Did Job's friends think he had the power to help himself (13)? On the contrary, Job asserts that he has no help or resources in himself, neither does he have any hope to go on living. Success has been taken away from him; consequently, he feels he has lived long enough and it is time to go to see his Redeemer.

C. Job expresses his disappointment in his friends (6:14-23)
Job had expected that his three companions would have showed him 'kindness' (Hebrew, *hesed*, 'loyal love'), but these three so-called 'friends' 'withheld' such 'loyal love.' When they took that course of action, they also thereby forsook 'the fear of the Almighty' (14b), comments Job.

In Job's view, his three friends were more like an unreliable riverbed, which on the one hand was filled with torrents of water when the ice melted upstream off the mountain tops, but which on the other hand vanished away and became nothing but dry beds or empty wadis in the summer, when their water was most needed (15-17). Such undependability matched the disappointing ways of Job's three friends – they too could be just as undependable as they outwardly pretended to be concerned, but became as untrustworthy as a dried up riverbed (15).

The camel caravans from Tema and Sheba in northern Arabia often in the summer and dry season had to abandon the old paths of the riverbeds to search for water throughout the vast wasteland (18-19), which often resulted in their getting lost, disappointed, and confused (20). In the same way, the three of these counselors had become such poor sources of hope and strength to Job (21). They had acted cowardly towards Job, for when they saw his appearance and heard of his losses, they showed no empathy or sympathy for Job. Instead, they decided he had been judged by God. But Job had not tried to bribe them to get a positive decision from a judge or asked of any of the three of them to pay a ransom for him (22), so he could be freed from some enemy. They had never been asked to financially stake Job, so he could have been rescued from the grasp of any ruthless aggressors of Job or his stuff (23). It seemed as if they were afraid of getting too close to Job and his issues lest they would become too involved.

D. Job makes a plea to his three 'comforters'/counselors (6:24-30)
Now that Job has told his three counselors that they have deeply disappointed him, he pleads with them to point out just where he has gone off the tracks with God. If they

could teach him and point out where he has gone wrong and sinned, Job could benefit from such views if they were honest words (24-25a). However, their words would prove nothing, for such words from these men were more like a lot of wind (26).

Job lays down the challenge: 'Would I lie to you?' (28). Please, gentlemen, Job continues to urge, don't be unfair and unjust. You are playing with my reputation and integrity. Look at me, Job adds, for there is no wickedness on my lips. Anyway, don't you think I can detect malice that exists on your part? (30).

E. Job describes his misery (7:1-6)
Job is not finished complaining, for once again he launches into a further description of his miserable state. Once more, as he did in chapter 3, Job likens his situation to that of a man who is more like a hired hand (7:1). This man works in the hot sun and longs for the evening to come (2a), when he will be paid for his work and escape the heat of the sun (2b). But life is filled with a lot of labor and toil with only a slight hope for some respite from the daily grind.

But Job declares that his situation is even worse than that, for ever since his suffering began he has had months of emptiness and futility (3). His nights seemed to be too long, as the night dragged on filled with his tossing and turning until the dawn came (4). At least hired hands and slaves could rest and sleep at night, but Job felt his suffering had deprived him of even this pleasure.

On the other hand, Job's days went flying by all too quickly, like the shuttle on a weaver's beam – all of this without any hope of being rescued (6). Meanwhile, his skin was covered with worms and hardened, his open sores formed scabs and pus oozed from his infected body (5).

F. Job prays to God (7:7-21)

Since Job prayed that he might die and not live in chapter 3, there may be a slight possibility that now his trust in God is beginning to increase somewhat, for now he prays that God would remember his life. True, Job viewed his life as 'but a breath' (7a), or a cloud that vanishes (9), for when he died he would not return to his house (10). Instead, he would go 'down to the grave' and 'not return.' (9). But at least in death he would be released from the inspecting and searching eyes of God (7-8).

After Job talks to the Lord about how short and brief life is, he lets go with an outburst of his anguish, not holding back very much as he bitterly complains to God: 'Am I some sort of sea monster that you have put me on such a close watch and inspection?' he exclaims (12). Some think Job may have been alluding to the Canaanite Ugaritic myth, in which the sea god Yam was overcome by Baal, or perhaps he referred to the Babylonian myth, where the god Marduk defeated the sea monster Tiamat. But Job was not giving credibility to the truthfulness of either these myths, even though he may have been borrowing the language from them to describe his own condition. His speech is somewhat out of control, for Job does accuse God of scaring him to death in his dreams, so that even his sleep was disturbed (13-14). This causes Job to lapse back again into a request that God would allow him to suffocate (or be strangled) in death (15). Therefore, he begs for God to leave him alone (16b). Commentators note that verses 17-18 are similar to Psalm 8:4; but whereas in the Psalm, the psalmist expresses a glad surprise for God's concern, in Job's case he feels haunted by God's close inspection of him every morning (17-18). He would have preferred to have God look away from him and to let him alone (19). That's what he wanted!

Job now uses the word 'sin' for the first time in this book as he asks God, 'Tell me if I have sinned.' (20). Job feels as if God has made him His 'target' (20b). Even if God thought that Job had sinned, why hadn't God forgiven him (21)? Here Job uses all three common words for sin: 'sin,' 'transgression,' and 'iniquity.' (20-21). In fact, Job feels that God is harassing him and this leads him to long for his own death.

2. FACING BILDAD'S BLUNT AND IMPOLITE SCOLDING (8:1-22)

If Eliphaz had begun his speech in a polite and gentle way, Bildad came on to Job with a series of blunt and discourteous charges and accusations. Bildad was sure he knew what Job's problem was; or, so he thought he knew: Job had sinned; if he would repent of his sin, he would no doubt recover his losses as soon as he acknowledged his wrong doing. Nothing else would help Job except this action before God!

Bildad launches right into his attack on Job without any kind words or polite acknowledgements of any kind. Bildad boldly and bluntly asks Job: 'How long will you say such things ... [that are full of] blustering wind?' (8:2). Bildad is really angry with Job, for if Job was suffering, when he had done no wrong (as he claimed), then what could happen to Bildad and the rest of his friends in the future, if Job was telling it like it was? Consequently, Job just had to be full of a lot of hot air and false theology! Job was suffering, so there had to be some sin present, or at least that is how they saw the issue!

But Bildad has another question: 'Does God pervert justice?' (8:3). Bildad wants Job to know that if he claims he has not sinned, even when such heaps of grief and pain have visited him, then Job's suffering would count as evidence against God's fairness in that God would have 'pervert[ed]' the moral order of the universe – which was an impossibility; for, of course, God would never pervert anything! Moreover, Bildad cruelly goes on to score even more points against Job when he points out that Job's children must also have sinned, for that is why they suffered the penalty they received for their sin (8:4). Wow, now the gloves are off and Bildad is going for the knockout punch. This is hitting a man while he is down and hitting him where it hurts! However, there is hope for Job, Bildad finally allows, if he would 'seek God earnestly' (5) and he would become 'pure and upright,' God, no doubt, would 'rouse himself on [Job's] behalf' (5-6).

The source of Bildad's theology, he asserts, is to be found in the sayings of the forefathers (8). He wants Job to compare his case against those found in history and with previous generations, for in that case, Job would see what his ancestors had learned, and he would see how brief life was. Why life was but a 'shadow,' and it was as if we were only born just 'yesterday' (8-9). Thus, we really knew 'nothing,' for we were all Johnnies come lately! (9a).

In order to emphasize the precariousness of our lives, Bildad uses two illustrations from the life experience of plants: the papyrus plant and reeds (11-13). Neither one can grow without water; therefore, in the same way neither can the wicked be sustained without the grace and forgiveness of God (13). That is what is wrong with Job, Bildad charges: he has forgotten, or perhaps deliberately decided not to confess his sin to God.

When mortals forget God, then any hope of receiving help begins to fail them (13) and their trust begins to crumble as it becomes as fragile as relying on a spider's web (14). Bildad was insinuating that Job had rested his security on his possessions, but that was equal to clinging to a spider's web for security.

Another illustration Bildad employs is again from botany (16-19), where a thriving plant may do well in the sunshine and with generous watering of it; however, if it is uprooted and torn from the original place where it was planted, then its life will wither away and other plants will take the place from which it was uprooted (19). Bildad's point is this: Job has been uprooted from his possessions and prosperity, therefore others would arrive to take the space left from which he had been uprooted.

Triumphantly Bildad concludes his speech to Job in verses 20-22 by affirming that God will never reject one who is blameless, nor will God, on the other hand, ever show His favor to evil-doers (20). But if Job will repent of his sin, as Bildad has suggested, then he will again be filled with laughter and joy (21), as his enemies will experience shame and their dwellings will be no more (22). Job, he seemed to caution: remember bad guys never win; they always lose; don't be a bad guy!

3. JOB ANSWERS BILDAD (9:1–10:22)

A. The awesomeness of God (9:1-12)

Bildad's remarks were so beside the mark that Job decides to ignore them for the present and focus instead on the greatness of God. Job was just as aware of the majesty and greatness of God as were Bildad and his friends, but perhaps the question Eliphaz had posed in his famous dream vision was still on the top of Job's mind: 'How can mere mortals prove their innocence before God?' (9:2b; cf. 4:17). But for Job, the biggest question in his mind is : How could he present his case for unfair suffering before God? Was God indeed arbitrary, for if Job was an 'upright man,' but he still could not find a way of making his case before God, what hope was there for anyone else?

Job proceeds to answer his own question by suggesting several reasons why it appears to be useless to pretend that any of us are on such a par with God that we could present our case before God:

1. Who could answer God in a dispute with Him; He who is so mighty? (3). It just did not seem feasible at all. The gap between God and mortals is too great!

2. Who has resisted God's power and His wisdom? (4). What He has decreed stands firm, and that is that!

3. Who is capable of moving mountains and shaking the earth as God is? (5-6). No one could match that kind of power or simulate His wisdom.

4. Who can make the sun shine and make the constellations to come into being except the Lord – and He did it simply by the word of His mouth (7-9).

God cannot be forced by anyone, including Job, to describe what He is doing (12). He was, and continues to be, incomparably great, but He also is incomprehensible (11). Indeed, he had made the Big Dipper in the north (the 'Bear'), Orion in the south, Pleiades in the east and west and the constellations in the south (9). Mortals are not on His level at all.

B. *The overwhelming presence of God (9:13-24)*

Job feels that God is so angry with him that God would not turn back His anger (13). Why even the monster Rahab crouched down in front of the Lord God. Rahab was another name for the god Tiamat or Leviathan, but here this name was used as a figure for the force of evil. But if this force could not stand in the presence of God's anger, then what chance did Job have? (14). Job continues, even if he were innocent, he feels he could not answer God, for he does not think God would listen to him (15-16). God, in Job's view was bent on crushing him and overwhelming him (17-18). Moreover, God simply outclasses Job in strength and justice; God is just too strong for him! Since verses 13-18 had dealt with God's power, now verses 20-24 take up God's justice. Thus, so strong would the justice of God be evident that Job was afraid he would get all confused as he tried to make the case for his innocence before Him and therefore he would become a witness against himself (20). Furthermore, by now Job has come to the improper conclusion that it no longer makes a difference whether he is guilty or not: God would destroy the blameless person as well as the wicked one (22).

Surely it is such a sharp protest that comes from Job's lips that it constitutes a protest against all three of his 'comforters' – who had argued that God always blessed the good person, but only punished the evil ones (23-24). Job concludes that if it was not God who acted this way, then who was it (24c)? Job feels his own case refutes all claims to the contrary.

C. Job charges God with unfairness (9:25-35)

Job continues to lament his condition, for he cries out that God will not acquit him, no matter how hard he tries to get God involved in his case (9:25-35). Job goes on to further lament that God will not stop punishing him (10:1-7), neither will the Lord leave him alone (10:8-17), nor will He let him die, as he wants to (10:18-22).

Once again Job remarks on how quickly his days are flying by: they are swifter than a runner and faster than the Egyptian boats made of papyrus – the speedsters of that day (9:25-26)! Moreover, Job's days are accelerating to the speed of an eagle or falcon that could swoop down on its prey at speeds of up to 120 miles per an hour! (9:26b).

If Job tried to forget his problems as a means of cheering himself up, it was no use, for his pain would remind him otherwise, and God would nevertheless still hold him guilty (9:27-28). In fact, if God had already regarded Job as guilty, according to Job's way of accounting for things, then things like cleansing himself with soap, or his hands with lye soda, would not help at all. God would only plunge him into the slime pit or cesspool with the result that even his clothes would stink to high heaven (9:29-31). God just was 'not a man like [Job],' so that he could meet God in a court of arbitration (9:32). But Job still wished for a divine 'Arbiter,' or an 'Umpire,' a 'lawyer' who would mediate his case as he placed his hand on both Job and God (9:33). Perhaps this Mediator would remove the 'rod' of God's affliction from him and he would not be frightened by God any longer (9:34). However, Job sadly concludes that such a hope is outside the realm of reality, for he can not speak up without his being afraid of God; besides, that is just not the way things are! (9:35) – there is no Mediator or 'Daysman' available, and it does not appear that God would voluntarily step in to relieve him of his suffering. Was Job forgetting about the coming Messiah?

D. O that God would stop punishing me (10:1-7)

Since Job is without a Mediator, or so he thinks, he continues to assume the role of acting as his own defense attorney as he belly-aches: 'I loathe my very life' (10:1). But Job still wants to know what God's charges against him are (10:2b). Hearing none, Job determines instead of trying to rid himself of his complaints and trying to cheer his soul up, he would give 'free rein to [his] complaint' and 'speak out of the bitterness of [his] soul'(10:1b-c). In this new role, Job would really ask God why He was after him with his condemnations and sufferings (10:2b).

With that Job begins to pepper God with a whole list of questions. First of all, does God get a kick out of oppressing Job (3)? Is God going to spurn the work of His own hands

(3b)? Is God going to favor the wicked, as He seemed to be doing (3c)? Is the Lord using eyes, just as mortals use their eyes to spot faults (4a)? Surely God's days are not as short as are Job's own days, are they (5)? Job knows that God searches out his sin, but surely he also knows that he must have been innocent and not guilty, so why hasn't God sent anyone to rescue him(7)?

E. O God, do not let me be left to myself (10:8-17)

Why did God create Job's body in the first place; why did He spend so much labor in making him if He was going to destroy him (10:8)? Would the divine Maker now abandon and destroy him after going to all that trouble of making him (8b)? Hadn't God formed Job much as a potter shapes a vessel, so why would God smash him back into dust again (9)? The Lord had knitted Job together with bones and sinews, then clothed him with flesh in the womb of his mother (11), much like the process of curdling milk into cheese (10). Now if God had taken all that trouble to make Job, why then would He not now take notice of him and acquit him of the punishments that were coming over him and let him go free (12-14)?

Job could not understand why God seemed to be stalking him like one hunts for a lion (16). Instead, it appears as if God was raising up one new witness after another against Job (17). God's power swept over Job like one wave after another (17b).

F. O God let me die (10:18-22)

Job has had it. He returns to the theme he had raised in chapter 3 and again in Job 6:8-9. Why has God paid so detailed attention to His creation in the womb only now to destroy him? (18). Would Job not have been better off just dying in the womb? Surely it would have been better for him to have gone right from his mother's womb into the tomb of his grave (19). If only God would let him alone (20), then he would get a little peace and quiet before he went to his death (20-21). Job calls his grave the 'place of no return' (21a), 'the land of gloom and deep shadow,' 'the land of deepest night, of deep shadow and disorder, where even the light is like darkness' (21b-22). Usually, it is not wise to regard the thoughts of a despondent man, especially on the subject of death, as a source of theology. Here Job is all wrapped up in the concept of 'darkness' and 'gloom.' But Job still feels that the grave, which he called 'Sheol,' is a much better place to go to than his present state of being, Job is acting as if he were obsessed with the topic of death, for he had raised the topic in Job 3:21-22; 7:21; and now he repeats it in Job 10:21-22.

Conclusions

1. Bildad certainly did not bring out the best in Job; in fact his speech seemed to make Job long all the more intensely for a divine Mediator or Arbiter to intercede on his behalf.

2. Job thought he had more than a right to voice his complaint to God and ask Him, as he asked his three friends, to name what sins he had committed and ones that he may have left unconfessed before God.

3. Job told his friends that they were no comforters at all; instead, they were like dried up riverbeds that brought no relief to one who thirsted for help.

4. Despite all of Job's troubles, he still celebrated the majesty and greatness of God.

5. Job's gloomy reflections on the grave are understandable, but later he escaped the darkness and gloom of the pictures he used to characterize death earlier to assert that his eyes would one day look on his Redeemer (19:23-27).

QUESTIONS FOR REFLECTION
AND DISCUSSION

1. Was Job wrong to keep claiming that he was innocent of any guilt for sins he had not committed?

2. Why did his three friends insist so persistently on the fact that Job had to be guilty of unconfessed sin?

3. What do you think God was teaching Job, as well as Satan, during this time of suffering?

4. Who best fulfills the role of 'Mediator' or 'Arbiter' in Job 9:33? Is this an early expectation of the coming Messiah?

5. How does Eliphaz's earlier speech compare with that of Bildad's speech?

Chapter 4:
Job 11:1–14:22

Job argues with Zophar as he prepares to face the living God

(Job 11:1–14:22)

1. ZOPHAR'S FIRST SPEECH (11:1-20)

Zophar was the third so-called 'friendly' 'comforter' to counsel Job, but by this time our 'comforter' has become so infuriated with Job for his long-winded speeches and his insistence that he is innocent of any sins or wrong-doing before God that could serve as a reason for his suffering, that Zophar explodes and lets Job have it without any niceties or politeness of language. Eliphaz and Bildad had not exactly been all that delicate in the way they had expressed themselves either, but at least they had not been as insensitive, blunt, and as straightforward as Zophar now was.

A. Zophar rebukes Job for his speeches and theology (11:1-6)
Zophar the Naamathite charges Job with: (1) being too talkative (11:2), (2) with scoffing all three of his 'friends,' so that Job was left unrebuked by anyone of them (11:3), (3) with claiming to be 'flawless' and 'pure' in his teaching

(11:4), and (4) with being very obtuse and slow to learn from God what he should have known about the results of sin (5-6). Zophar is even more blunt and uncouth than Bildad. In fact, Zophar sarcastically wishes God would answer Job once and for all to shut him up and to show him what the three of them have been trying to help him with, by their teaching him what he persisted in rejecting (9:3, 16). Surely God would straighten Job out as He would certainly speak against Job for his sin and call him to repentance as all three of them had tried to do. What God would show Job would be the secret wisdom of His divine counsels (11:6). Moreover, the wisdom of God was double-sided; that is why some of that wisdom had perhaps eluded Job (11:5-6). Better still, it had to be said that God had been too good to Job, for he had gotten less punishment than he deserved, for this could easily be shown by the talkative way Job was expressing himself in front of his three friends.

B. Zophar focuses on God's inscrutable wisdom (11:7-12)
Instead of choosing to focus on God's 'justice,' as Eliphaz and Bildad had, Zophar chooses to speak on God's unbounded 'wisdom.' He depicts God's wisdom as that which is way out of the reach of man, for in its height, it exceeds the heavens, in its depths it goes further down than Sheol, in its length it is longer than the earth; yes, God's wisdom exceeds the breath of the seas (11:7-9). Of course, Zophar is correct, so far, but when he comes to applying this teaching to Job in what follows, he is way off base; in fact, he is definitely wrong and way out of line! Job had already said that no one could restrain God (9:12;

cf. 11:10), but Zophar disagrees with Job on his bad charge that God did not know the difference between the guilty and the innocent (9:22; cf. 11:11).

Despite Zophar's emphasis on the wisdom of God that could not be measured, he nevertheless involves himself in a contradiction. When Zophar claims that God's ways are unknowable and beyond any mortal's understanding, how then does Zophar come to know that God overlooked some of Job's sin (11:11)? Did Zophar have some secret access to God's unfathomable wisdom? He was obviously contradicting himself.

Zophar really goes way overboard in his pretense of knowing how stupid Job was. He quotes a proverb that says that the chances of an 'idiot' (presumably like Job) becoming wise are about the same as a wild donkey producing a man as its foal (11:12)! That's not nice at all! Wild donkeys may be more stupid than domesticated donkeys, but how did Zophar get so smart that he was able to assess Job's level of intelligence in comparison to these wild donkeys? It raises the question as to who is the real 'idiot' in this contest of speeches: Job or Zophar?

C. Zophar's recommendations to Job for his recovery (11:13-20)
Like his two colleagues, Zophar urges Job to turn his heart to the Lord in repentance, to pray by spreading his hands out to the Lord, and to put away sin from himself, which he had been allowing in his life, and instead, to allow no evil in his tent (11:13-14). Zophar promises that if Job would follow these steps, God would surely bless him so that: (1) he would be rid of any shame, (2) his conscience would be freed (15), (3) he would forget about all the trials

he had been carried through (16), and (4) his life would sparkle like the noonday and any residual darkness would become like the brightness of the morning (17). Job could once again enjoy security and hope and he would be able to rest in safety (18). No one would make him afraid and once again he would be sought out by others for his advice and favor (19). But over against all these blessings, if Job decided not to follow this advice, his eyes, like those of the wicked, would fail him, for then all possible escapes would elude him, and the hope of Job, or of the wicked, would be no more than a dying gasp (20).

Once again, Zophar, like the previous two speakers Eliphaz and Bildad, was right in saying that God brought blessing and hope to those who repented of their sin, but this only told half of the truth. Zophar was wrong when he forgot that God sometimes allowed suffering and pain for other reasons than for trying to get the attention of the sinner. Zophar was wrong in presuming that the only thing Job needed to do was to repent and then everything would be alright once more. Zophar, like his friends, failed to see what Job was facing and how he had to deal with it.

2. Job answers Zophar's speech (12:1–13:12)

Job was fed up with his three so-called 'friends,' for they kept hammering home one single point of their theology, which was that sin produces suffering; and since Job was suffering, he must repent if he was going to be happy again! Each counselor used a different source of authority to silence Job. Eliphaz used his dream as his basis of authority, but how was Job to refute someone else's dream? Bildad appealed to what the forefathers had taught from their experiences, but they were no longer alive, so how could Job answer them? Zophar chose to focus on the irrefutable wisdom of God, so how was Job to debate a point with which he agreed in principle anyway? Job was being pushed further and further into a corner by the three comforters, and thus he sunk into a deep depression over his mortal state and his inability to converse directly with God.

Therefore, Job divides his attention in half in this next section, for the first half he addresses his friends (12:1–13:19) and in the second half of his response he addresses his cause to God (13:20–14:22). Job's quandary was this: he just could not buy the cause-and-effect case for justice that his three buddies were making, but on the other hand, neither could he find a way to account for what had happened to him and to reckon that with the justice of God. He was stuck in a deep quandary.

A. Job refutes his three friends (12:1–13:19)
Job is sick and tired of all his three friends repeating back to him one after another. So, he begins with deep sarcasm: 'Surely [you three] are the people and wisdom will die with you' (12:2). Job felt so persecuted by this time that he was coming close to experiencing paranoia. For when your friends start calling you stupid and likening your intelligence to that of a wild donkey, it is time to let them know what you think about that. After all, he too was one of the wise men of the east, so what gave these three dudes the right to demean and belittle him? Job felt he was just as intelligent as they were, and not one whit inferior to them (12:3). Anyway, who didn't know the stuff they were

spouting off? It was part of the collected wisdom of all mortals of that day! So where did these three counselors get the nerve to infer that they had the monopoly on such divine knowledge. That counter attack by Job should have taken some of the wind out of their sails, for what they taught was merely common knowledge shared by the masses (3)!

Furthermore, the rigid case these three men were making for the justice of God just did not fit the common experience of mortals. First of all, Job volunteers: Take my case! (12:4). Job argues that he is 'righteous and blameless' (4c), yet you three so-called 'friends' have made me into nothing more than a 'laughingstock' (4). Mortals like you also make a 'laughingstock' out of other unfortunate souls 'whose feet slip' (12:5). So where is the justice if you show such disregard for those who are already down?

A second argument Job mounts is this: what about the robbers and bandits who hate God, yet they seem to prosper and feel secure? (12:6) A third argument can be added here, which was this: don't even the animals know that calamity comes from God (12:7-9)? Moreover, doesn't the ear test words and the mouth test food? (12:11) If so, then let these three arguments test the three of you as well, Job huffs!

Bildad had argued that wisdom was found among the aged (8:8). But Job now counters that earlier assertion (12:12) by calling attention to God's 'wisdom and might, his counsel and understanding' (12:13). Job of course knew God's wisdom was true teaching as did his friends, but what Job's three 'comforters' did not seem to know was that along with the retributive justice they prized so highly, and which they constantly advocated for Job, there were just as clear cases of evil robbers, which involves a kind of mysterious wisdom and a certain unpredictable evidence of the might and power of God that does not fit the category of retributive justice (12:14-15). When God with-holds the water from the earth, there is drought (15), but when He lets loose the floods, the waters can swamp the earth (15). God is in control of all things: both in matters involving the deceived and the deceiver (16). The point is this: No one can reverse the destructive powers of God, for if He tears something down, 'it cannot be rebuilt' (14).

Even well-established leaders, priests, nobles, and officials may seem strong and powerful on the face of things, but it is God who can and does both make some great and destroy others (17-21). Some are led off to captivity while others escape to freedom. In a similar way, God makes some nations great and yet He destroys other nations (23). Some nations our Lord 'enlarges,' yet He disperses others – all of this occurs as a result of His sovereign plan (23b). Some leaders are given wisdom by God and others are 'deprived of their reason' as He sends them out to live in the wastelands (24). They are without any direction or guidance as they grope around, searching for the light and as they stagger in their own drunkenness (25).

Job is scoring points with his interlocutors, for if everything in God's universe followed the pattern of retributive justice, then would not all of earth's leaders be blessed by God? But history also gives the lie to that assertion.

Job finds fault both with his friends' ability to help him theologically (13:15) and their attempts to represent God accurately (13:6-12). What his friends taught, Job had already heard (13:1), and what they knew, Job already knew too (13:2), so the three of them were basically worthless and without any value to a person hurting like Job. Job was not one whit inferior to these three purveyors of one-liners. He was just as able, and just as equipped, as they thought they were.

Job didn't want to hear more from these three dudes; he wanted to speak personally with the Almighty God (13:3). At least that would be a whole lot more productive than listening to the misguided charges of these men. They had just smeared [literally 'plastered'] Job and his reputation with lies (13:4); they were 'worthless physicians' (13:4b). They neither diagnosed Job's problem correctly, nor had they prescribed the correct antidote either. Job wished one thing from them: that they would be silent, which would finally show they had some wisdom! (13:5). They were not as wise as they thought themselves to be.

Job wanted them to be quiet so they could listen to his argument and hear the plea of his lips. (13:6-12). Job begins with three questions for his visitors. They are:

1. Do you speak so deceitfully about me for the benefit of God? (7).

2. Do you think that you are defending God's holy and righteous reputation when you argue with such partiality the case you think God has against me? (8).

3. Do you think if God examined each of the three of you that, you could deceive Him as easily as you apparently can deceive mere mortals? (9).

There is no doubt that God will certainly rebuke you if you 'secretly show partiality' (10), which is exactly what did happen to them when God intervened and showed the three of them the error of their ways in Job 42:7-8. They may have thought they were defending God, but in fact they were only defending one view of God and making sure no suffering would come to them except in a retributive sense. Nor did it occur to them that they should ask God for wisdom in applying God's teaching to the situation Job was in.

Never did Job deny God's justice, yet at the same time he upheld his own righteousness and purity, for Job was just as frank and as bold with the three of them, as especially Zophar had been with him. He asks, first of all, when God examines the three of you, will you not be terrified, and would not the dread of Him fall on each of you? (13:11), which is exactly what happened in the end (42:7). Job's assessment of all he has heard in this first round of speeches is this: 'Your maxims are proverbs of ashes; your defenses are defenses of clay.' (13:12).

3. JOB PRESENTS HIS CASE TO GOD (13:13–14:22)

A. Job is willing to risk his life, if he must, to state his case before God (13:13-19)
Job begins by demanding that his friends keep silent (13:13), as he had requested earlier in 13:5. Job is ready to state his case, come what may (13b). To be sure, Job knows that he might be risking his life if God does not accept him or his defense. The expression he uses is literally that he was 'taking [his] flesh in [his] teeth,' just as an animal likewise

risks losing its prey to other animals when it carried the prey's flesh around in its teeth (14). So, Job knows what he intends to do is filled with danger – especially in his deep desire to speak directly with God. However, this sufferer was bound and determined to talk with God, even if it meant he might lose his own life. As Job put the matter: 'Though he slay me, yet will I hope in him; I will surely defend my ways to his face' (15). Despite the familiar ring these words raise for most Christian readers, the Hebrew is not as easily rendered as this translation has it. This verse 15 might better be rendered:[1] 'If [God] slays me, I will not tremble, provided that I [can] argue my case before him.' The point is that Job wishes to argue the case of his innocence before God at any, and all, costs! And since no godless person would dare to present himself before God's tribunal for divine vindication, this was another indication that Job was innocent (16), for why would he risk exposure if he knew he was guilty?

Job requests that his case be listened to carefully so that all understand his explanation of his case (17). Job had assembled his arguments much as a defense attorney would marshal his arguments, for he confidently knew he was right in all the contentions that pertained to his suffering and that if fairly treated, it would result in his vindication (18). He felt his arguments were so strong that he would easily win (18b), whereas previously he did not have the same high degree of confidence. Previously he had said: 'I know that you will not acquit me' (9:28b). Moreover, Job

---

1. As rendered and better argued by E. Dhorme, A *Commentary on the Book of Job*. Transl. by Harold Knight, (Nashville:Thomas Nelson Publishers, 1984), p. 187.

felt that no one would be able to bring accurate charges that would lead to their proving that guilt could be found against him (19).

B. Job presents his case to God (13:20-28)

Job asks God mainly for two things: (1) 'Withdraw your hand from me' and 'stop frightening me with your terrors' (21). Routinely, Job in each of his replies to his three friends had also addressed God: Job turned to God when he replied to Eliphaz (7:12-21). He again turned to God when he replied to Bildad (9:28-33; 10:2-19), as he did so when he replied also to Zophar (13:20-14:22). The Lord God was the One he really wanted to talk to and hear from rather than from these three miserable comforters!

Job did not care who spoke first, whether God or him; the main thing was that he could get-on-line with his Lord (22). But hearing no word from the Lord, Job begins by speaking up first. He initiates his speech by asking God: 'Show me my offense and sin' (23b); specify my wrongs and the sins I have committed (23a). However, the silence that ensues from heaven only makes Job ask why God is hiding His face and why He is acting as if Job were His enemy (24). Why is God treating Job as if he were little more than a leaf tossed about in the wind or just dry chaff (25)? As Job saw it, God was writing down bitter things against him as He brought up to the surface the sins of his youth, and Job thought this was really unfair of God (26). If God continued to fail to interact with Job, then why was He treating Job like His prisoner, shackling him so that he was unable to discover what was going on and what was wrong (27)?

Job felt like he was 'decaying like a rotten thing' or like a 'garment that was moth-eaten' (28). Job could not figure out why God was picking on him when he was so weak, valueless, broken, and wasting away!' Why was God persecuting him? Job was in the depths of despair.

C. Job was melancholic but note his solid hope (14:1-22)
God's failure to meet with Job on his human terms causes him to suddenly let loose bold assertions such as the claim that he could win a case for his own righteousness and purity in a court with God. But such poor bravado leads him to sink into a morbid mood as he begins to flirt with hopelessness in 14:1-6.

Job was stuck on the horns of a dilemma. If God would not answer him, then how could he argue the case he was so confident would vindicate his position of innocence? (13:13-28). And if God could not be subpoenaed to appear in court, life was over for Job and death probably was certain. Accordingly, Job begins his jeremiad by saying: 'Man born of woman is of few days and full of trouble' (14:1). Since a woman is frail, then so too was the fruit of her womb frail and weak. To add to the problem of humanity's brevity and shortness of days, these days were also 'determined' and fixed, so that God knew the number of months each would get (14:5). Thus, mortals seemed to 'spring up like flower[s],' but they also tended to 'wither' and did not 'endure' (2). It was just such a defenseless creature that God would judge (14:3). In light of such facts, 'who could bring what is pure from the impure?' (14:4).

If man was so ephemeral, yet so corralled by God, why would God want to look on him anyway? (14:6). Man was here on earth to put in his time like an employee who punched in on the clock and punched out when time or work was finished.

However, Job sees a similarity between a tree sprouting again after it has been cut down (14:7, as some tended to do) and a man's 'renewal' or 'sprouting' again after he dies (14:14). Some trees will sprout new shoots alongside the trunk of the cut down tree (14:7b), yet when it detects the presence of water, some trees may spring back to life again by sending out new shoots! And even if its roots may dry up and its original stump may decay in the meantime (14:8), it will once again ultimately bud like a plant at the scent of water (9).

The situation with a man dying at first appears to be different from that of a tree (10), for a mortal breathes his last and is no more (10). This mortal lies down in death and appears to rise no more, or be roused from his sleep again (12), but Job goes on to wish it were possible that Sheol, which is here used as the word for the 'grave,' would limit his time in the grave until God's anger had expired, just as man's time on earth is limited (13). So, what is the answer? If a person dies, will that person live again? (14a)? Job responds: 'All the days of my service I will wait until my renewal/sprouting comes' (14b). Most people miss the point that Job uses the root of the same Hebrew word he had used on the tree in 14:7 (*halif,* 'to sprout afresh,' or 'spring to life' again in verse 7 and *Halifah,* 'relief,' 'change,' 'sprouting' in verse 14). Job holds out the prospect of a resurrected life in the future while one was waiting in this life for the change and relief that would arrive from God,

91

much as one platoon of soldiers was 'replaced' or 'relieved' by another platoon of soldiers.

Job is sure that one day God would summon him to court as the Lord God would 'long for the creature [his] hands had made (15).' God would experience deep emotional longing for Job. When that happens, Job and God would enjoy beautiful fellowship, as God counted [Job's] daily steps, but '[God] would not keep track of his sin' (16). God would seal up Job's transgression so that all the evidence gathered against him would be put out of God's sight and 'wrapped up' or 'plastered over' (17).

Job pulls together four metaphors from nature to describe how God destroys a frail man's hope (Hebrew word for man here is `enosh, 'weak man,' i.e., a 'frail man') (18-19). These metaphors are: (1) like crumbling or eroding mountains, (2) like a rock moving from its otherwise stationary place, (3) like water wearing away the stones as it washes over them, and (4) like torrents of water washing away the soil. God has the power to over-run the existence of mortals and send each away (20). As a result of the death of this man, he does not see his sons honored (21) and his body feels the pain of death and corruption (22).

Conclusions

Once again Job concludes his response to Zophar, as he has in each of the first cycle of three speeches with his friends, on a somewhat despondent note about death. Job had felt that the value and worth of his three friends' speeches amounted to less than nothing. But what he longed for was not to hear any explanations from his friends; he wanted instead to have a conversation with God. God knew his heart and He knew how he had tried to live for Him. But what Job could not understand was why was God allowing such a use of His power to afflict him when it all seemed so unfair and so uncalled for.

Zophar's speech was much too inflexible to match the divine justice Job would or could attribute to God. But if Zophar and his two buddies were incorrect in their insistence on the retributive justice of God applied to Job, then what, or who, would explain Job's case?

QUESTIONS FOR REFLECTION
AND DISCUSSION

1. What was it in Zophar's speech that incited the anger of Job against him and his two buddies? Did Job, or do Christians in similar situations, ever have the right to get angry?

2. What did Zophar appeal to as the basis of his authority? Compare the grounds of authority appealed to by Eliphaz and Bildad.

3. What points did Job include in the case he drafted for his appearing before and facing God with his case for his innocence?

4. Was the content of the speeches of the three men true or false? If any parts of them were true, then what was so bad or deserving of the rebuke of God in Job 42:7-8?

5. What purpose did these three men serve in Job's suffering as God allowed them to harass Job? How does that figure into our Christian view of pain, grief and suffering? Do such actions by others have any functional part in our suffering?

The Second Cycle

Chapter 5:
Job 15:1–17:16

Eliphaz takes on Job a second time and Job responds

(Job 15:1–17:16)

The second cycle or round of ash-heap sessions between Job and his three visitors, Eliphaz, Bildad, and Zophar, appears in Job chapters 15–21. Heretofore, the three interlocutors have refused to advocate anything less than the fact that Job was experiencing pain and suffering simply because of his unconfessed sin. They stubbornly refused to consider or include in their theology any other explanation for Job's condition: in their view it had to be the way they viewed it, because Job persisted in claiming he was innocent, while he obviously must have sinned and had thus far refused to confess that sin.

But even these three men have tired of the monotony of insisting that Job had to repent of his sin, accordingly they no longer hold out an invitation for Job to confess his guilt in this second round of discussions. They have just plain given up on challenging Job any longer to admit his unconfessed sin: they must have figured he was never going to repent of any sin anytime soon. Instead, they begin to focus on what are the prospects and the future for the 'wicked' ones, such as Job surely illustrated. For example, Eliphaz stresses that the wicked were persons who were really endangered and in deep distress (chapter 15). Meanwhile, Bildad stresses the point that the wicked were trapped by their own deeds and were, as a result of that, forgotten by God (chapter 18). But Zophar again takes the lead in being the most dramatic and the one most brutally frank as he unmercifully notes (with Job as the obvious brunt of his point) that the wicked do not live very long on this earth, for they also lose their wealth as certainly as Job had experienced precisely that same sad fate (chapter 20)!

Job's so-called 'friends' heartlessly aim their pointed questions at him, but they do not ask him these questions in order to hear, or to ponder his answers, they ask instead only to unload their total frustration on Job and voice their disgust with him. Thus, Eliphaz sarcastically poses this question to Job: 'Do you listen in on God's council?' (15:8); i.e., are you party and privy to what goes on in heaven? How wise do you think you are, Job? Eliphaz is no less indignant and brutish in his new questioning, for he also wants to know: 'Why are we considered … stupid in your sight?' (18:3). Zophar, as usual, however, takes the cake, when he charges: 'I am greatly disturbed. I hear a rebuke that dishonors me' (20:2b-3a). Such accusations hardly seemed to constitute the words and sympathies of 'comforters,' or those whose mission started out as being one of consoling Job.

A. Eliphaz rebukes Job for his hot-air speeches (15:1-16)
To Eliphaz's way of thinking, Job has unwisely spewed forth a multitude of empty words on the three of them

that are useless and without any value whatsoever (15:2-3). In the light of such hot-air talk, how could Job claim he was wise or among the wise men of that day? (15:2). Job's speeches were just plain irreverent, and these speeches undermined one's devotion to God (15:4). Furthermore, Job's sin and guilt were prompting his mouth to speak so incautiously against God (5). Eliphaz asserts that he did not need to cast any accusations against Job, for Job's own words served that purpose very well (6).

Eliphaz by now is getting really fed up with Job and really hot under the collar, for who in the world does Job think he is anyway? Had he been the first man ever born? Was he the one who had made the hills? (7) Was he privy to what went on in the councils of God? (8a) Was wisdom limited to him alone? (8b). What did Job think he knew that the three of them did not know? (9).

Eliphaz is not being fair at all, for Job had not made such outrageous claims. He had merely claimed that his knowledge was on a par with the three of them, but he never claimed his understanding exceeded theirs (12:3; 13:2). Eliphaz, however, claimed that 'The gray haired and the aged are on our side, men even older than [Job's] father' (10). So where did Job get the chutzpah and sheer nerve to challenge their theology? Shouldn't he show more respect for the elderly?

Eliphaz seems to imply that his earlier speech in round one had words of consolation in it as he reminds Job of the way God acts (5:17-27), but Job does not seem to think very much of Eliphaz's words either or apparently of God's acts (11-13). Eliphaz charges Job with flashing his eyes at them and with letting his heart carry him away so that he vented his rage against God (12-13). But Eliphaz himself could not claim he had acted properly in speaking to Job, for he was speaking most irrationally and emotionally as he asserted incorrectly that Job had changed his spirit to act against God.

Eliphaz goes back over parts of his first speech (4:17), as if Job had not understood what he had said, by stressing that human beings born of women are impure and unrighteous (14). Moreover, if the heavens themselves are impure, then how is it that Job could claim that he, a mere mortal, who is 'vile (literally, "repulsive") and corrupt (literally, "sour like milk"), and who drinks up evil like water,' think he was pure before God? (15-16; cf. Eliphaz's earlier point in 4:18). Job, don't you know that you too are impure, repulsive, unrighteous, detestable, and corrupt, gulping down evil and sin as if they were water! Your suffering stems from nothing other than your corrupt nature and acting.

B. Eliphaz points to the punishment of the wicked (15:17-35)
Eliphaz is still resorting to his earlier observations, and his emphasis on what he had seen, as the basis for his comments. Thus, he begins in 15:17 – 'I will explain to you ... what I have seen' (cf. 4:8). But Eliphaz also supplements what he has seen with what the 'wise men had declared,' which had not been infected with the views of others (18-19). That teaching was this: the wicked suffer because of their sin (20). In fact, the wicked have trouble literally piled up for them (20b). The wicked also are terrified by the haunting feeling of the prospect that terror is all around them (21a). They think they

are now in a time of peace when suddenly such wicked persons are blindsided by the destroyer, just as Job had been vulnerable to the destroyer (21b). There seemed to be no return from the darkness and gloom of a guilty conscience, for the wicked were constantly tormented by their fear that misfortune would overtake them, and they would be designated to be on the wrong end of the sword (22). The wicked were left to wander about for food (23), as distress and anguish overwhelmed them (24). All the troubles listed in verses 20-24 as judgments for the wicked are now assigned reasons for their appearance in verses 25-26. It is because the wicked have 'shak[en their] fist[s] at God and vaunt[ed them]selves against the Almighty' (25). Such gestures of defiance Eliphaz thought fitted Job's defiance of God precisely. But here again Eliphaz has once again twisted what Job had said in 7:20 and 13:24. Eliphaz charges Job, as he already had in Job 15:13 with turning against God in his spirit (15:26). But that too was untrue of Job!

Eliphaz has another accusation against Job: Job had piled up luxuries for himself to luxuriate in (27), for according to the idiom of that day, fat persons often symbolized overly indulgent persons (Ps. 73:7; 119:70; Jer. 5:28),[1] and the wicked lived in ruined cities and rebuilt houses disregarding the curses that had often been placed on those same places (13:28; cf. Josh. 6:26; 1 Kings 16:34).[2] Job easily fitted that description as well, claimed Eliphaz.

---

1. Roy Zuck, *Job*, (Chicago: Moody Press, 1978), p. 74.

2. Ibid.

Eliphaz has one more charge left for Job in addition to the two charges he has already made. In verses 29-35 he attacks Job's alleged wealthy style of living and his fraudulent conduct. Therefore, Job's affluence and his rich opulence have been doomed to fail, as his present position demonstrated. (29). 'He will not escape darkness' (30a), as even his crops will dry up, as God sends what is called here the 'breath of God's mouth': but what was in actuality nothing less than the miserable hot east sirocco winds (30b-c). Job was relying only on what was empty and unreal, for it would all come to a tragic end (31-32a). Job's palm branches would no longer be green, and his grapes would drop their unripened fruit (32b-33). Hasn't Job learned yet, Eliphaz triumphantly observes, that going with the company of the godless was as pointless and barren as depending on nothing at all (34)? Job's stuff will all go up in flames, implies Eliphaz (34b). Wicked persons actually suffer huge losses when you really get down to thinking about it. They may dream up trouble and give rise to evil and deceit (35), but to what end? Look where it terminated!

1. JOB REPLIES TO ELIPHAZ A SECOND TIME (16:1–17:16)

A. Job expresses disgust for his three friends (16:1-5)
Eliphaz's merciless diatribe really ticked Job off. Eliphaz had said nothing that Job had not heard before! (16:2) In fact, the three of these alleged friends were nothing but 'miserable comforters' (2b). These three dudes did not bring solace or comfort, as they supposed themselves to be bringing; they brought nothing but trouble and mischief.

What on earth ailed the three of them, anyway, Job asks out loud (3b). They seem so irritated and so bent on making these windy speeches, rather than giving comfort and solace to Job (3a).

Job declares that had their positions been reversed, he could pile up similar words and mockingly shake his head at them too (4), but instead he would rather encourage them and use his words to bring comfort to them, had their fortunes been reversed (5).

B. Job makes his complaint against God (16:6-17)

For Job, no matter which way he went, whether he spoke, or he was quiet, his pain did not go away (6). What is more, despite the added trials the three supposed comforters brought, they however were not what was wearing him down; it was what was being handed out to him by God (7). God was wearing him down by taking away his strength and 'snatching away' or 'grabbing' his entire household (7). As a result, Job's friends viewed all this as evidence that he had sinned. Even Job's own emaciated body became another witness against him that he had sinned grievously against God (8).

Job boldly lamented God's brutal treatment of him as that of a savage beast that had assailed (Hebrew, *satam*, 'hate actively,'[3]) him, torn at his flesh, and snarled at him, while fixing a glassy stare on him and showing its teeth in defiance of him personally (9). As if this were not enough, Job's anguish was increased by all those who passed by

---

3. A point made by John E. Hartley, *The Book of Job*, NICOT, (Grand Rapids: Eerdmans, 1988), p 260. A word 'which is similar in sound to, if not directly related to, Hebrew *Satan*, 'prosecutor, Satan.'

the ash-heap where he had taken up his station in life, which was outside the city. All who passed by this ash-heap gaped at him with wide open mouths, obviously expressing contempt and disdain for him, and for what had happened to him (10). They even slapped the cheeks of Job's face in bitter contempt for him as they taunted him mercilessly (10b-c). The reason Job had become such an obvious target for scorn was that God had turned him over to these vicious ruffians (11). Things were getting worse rather than better!

Job's language moves up to a crescendo in 12-14 with word pictures that contrast his former state of well-being with the violence of the divine attack on his life. God has seized Job by the nape of his neck and crushed him (12b). It seems as if God has set Job up as a target for His arrows as they penetrated his kidneys and ripped open his gall (13b-c). God was like a warrior bursting through a wall as He rushed against Job (14).

As a result of God's huge assault against him, Job sewed up some sackcloth over his 'scabby skin' and 'buried his brow in the dust' (15). Sackcloth was the traditional garment worn by those who were grieving over some pending, or already experienced, major loss or affliction. In Job's case, it seems the garment had to be sewn together to actually fit Job's contorted figure as a result of his affliction. Moreover, Job's face was 'red with weeping' (16a) and deep shadows now outlined his eyes (16b). Yet all this happened, Job contended, even though he had done no violence and his prayer had been pure (17). Where was God and when would He show up for Job?

C. Job calls for a heavenly intercessor (16:18-21)
Job does not want his case to be covered over, so he appeals to the earth not to cover the blood from his affliction (18a), for even if he died before he had been vindicated, Job wants the evidence left on earth, so the injustice of his situation would finally be resolved. But Job also appeals to heaven for a 'Witness' to come to his aid and act as his defender (19-21). Did Job think this heavenly defender would be an angel, or even some other heavenly creature? No, he was appealing to God Himself to come from heaven to vindicate him. Job wants no one less than Messiah, a Mediator, to tell him what is going on. If it is thought that God could not act as a 'Witness' against Himself, as Job seemed to imply, then this objection has not considered the sheer drama that exists in the antinomy between God's justice expressed in His wrath against sin and yet at the same time His love for sinners that extends to those same sinners who surely did not deserve such love! Job is sure that this 'Advocate is on high' (19b) and that this 'Intercessor is [his] friend' (20a). Job's 'Intercessor,' he thinks, would argue his case before God the Father exactly as human beings act as friends for one another. Job notes in verses 21-22 the urgency of his appeal to his 'Witness'. If his request is not granted, he will perish in dishonor, for the end of his life is fast approaching.

D. Job calls on God to post bond and appear for him in court (17:1-16)
Job begins by emotionally collecting his grief and suffering in three short jeremiads in 17:1 – 'My spirit (here perhaps: the desire for life) is broken,' 'My days are cut short,' and

'The grave awaits me.' Added to all this grief is the fact that the 'mockers' surrounded him (2) and their hostile shouts moved Job to tears (2b). Job's only recourse is to plead with God to put up a surety or pledge for him, for to whom else could he go for such a guarantee? (3). With God posting this kind of bond for Job, while he waited for a heavenly court to process his case, Job felt relief might be on the way to him. Surely God knew that Job's friends were unwilling to post bail for him, for God Himself had closed the minds of his three friends so they could not see just what the facts were in Job's case (4). Anyway, God would never let Job's three friends triumph over him. Therefore, Job addresses the three of them by telling them that they were in deep trouble if their accusations turned out to be false, even to the point of the judgment passing on to their children (5). The penalty for giving false witness in the Bible had always been regarded as a serious crime that carried extremely grave consequences. So, the three so-called 'comforters' should watch their step!

Job goes on to describe how seriously he had been humiliated among his compatriots; in fact, he had become a 'byword' for all in his town and he was hated to the point of being a man people who were just passing by would spit at (6). Moreover, his eyes were blurry from all his weeping and his whole body was but a shadow of its former self (7).

One would expect such abuse against innocent victims from the ungodly, but such actions would appall the upright person (8). The person who is righteous, however, holds firmly to his way and as a result his hands are strengthened (9). Therefore, Job urges his three visitors to try harder to argue for their position, but so far Job has not been able to find a wise man among any of his three comforters (10). They are purveyors of grief and not solace!

As Job comes to the end of his lament over his situation in verses 11-16, he lapses back into musing on how gloomy and dark is death as his days go flying by (11). What he had laid out as his 'plans' all came undone, as had the 'desires of his heart' (11). But the friends who were supposed to bring Job comfort had promised that 'light was near' (12). At times they were full of cheery bromides, but they lacked any certainty to advocate what Job needed most from them.

But Job wasn't buying any of their syrupy talk. He was too occupied with the persistent conflict between the certainty of his death and the hope he likewise held on to dearly (13). Job argued that his home was marked out to be the grave, which he likened to a house, in which 'corruption' was his father and the 'worm' was his mother' (13-14). That raised the key question for Job: 'Where then is my hope?' Would Job go down to the grave and descend into the dust? (16). Was that to be the end of it all? The answer to that question must wait for more discussion.

Conclusions

1. Eliphaz had become more stringent and insistent in his depiction of the 'wicked,' so that Job might be frightened, I suppose, into coming around to his point that he should repent of his sin.

2. Eliphaz began to hint at the fact that Job's wealth had spoiled him as he depended more on his possessions than he did on God. That, then, was a key reason why God was afflicting him. But the text of Scripture gave no indication that this was a problem for Job.

3. Eliphaz was beginning to run out of explanations for Job's situation as he began trying every possible cause for such affliction, but it continued to miss the mark in Job's case by a country mile.

4. Job, however, without cursing God as Satan had bet he would, did depict God as a savage beast and One who abandoned him to brutal ruffians who besmirched Job's hard-earned reputation with all these insults and accusations.

5. Job longed for a heavenly Witness who would act as his Advocate and vindicate him. This hunger for a Mediator fully anticipated the need for a God-Man; One who stood between God and man and who would rescue and redeem mortals from attacks from the evil one, in other words a Messiah.

QUESTIONS FOR REFLECTION
AND DISCUSSION

1. Do you think Job in his distress had hit on precisely what our Lord Jesus would fulfill in His future redemptive role for mortals in His first and second coming when Job called for a 'Witness' and an 'Arbitrator' from on high?

2. How could God Himself lay down bail and a guarantee for Job since God was in heaven and Job was on earth?

3. How do you explain Job's moving back and forth between seeing God as being a Judge of all mortals and yet extending hope for all who trusted in Him?

4. What made Eliphaz so mad that he lashed out against Job so severely and violently? Did it have anything to do with how God might deal with him or his buddies, if God so chose?

5. If some of the things that Eliphaz said were true, then why did God say he and his friends had not spoken of the divine person what was accurate as it related to Job (42:7)?

6. Satan had his purpose in the suffering he had been causing, but what purpose did God have for Job and for us in what He was allowing to happen here?

Chapter 6:
Job 18:1–21:34

Bildad's and Zophar's second speeches and Job's certainty that he will see God again

(Job 18:1–21:34)

1. BILDAD'S SECOND SPEECH (18:1-21)

A. Bildad denounces Job's utterances (18:1-4)

Bildad begins his second speech by indignantly blasting Job for the long-winded and wordy speeches he has served up for all three of his comforters. Moreover, all three of them complained the same way: Job had treated them as if they were 'stupid' and no more than 'cattle' (18:3). However, there was not much that could be said for Bildad's speech; it was little more than a rehash of what Eliphaz had said in his second speech. Thus, Bildad merely parrots back to Job many of the identical subjects Eliphaz had already brought up to Job. For example, Bildad reiterates these themes from Eliphaz:[1]

THE SUBJECT	ELIPHAZ TEXT	BILDAD TEXT
Darkness comes to the wicked	15:22-23, 30	18:5-6, 18
The wicked dry up like plants	15:30b, 32-33	18:16

---

1. This list is essentially the same as that given by Roy Zuck, p. 81.

THE SUBJECT	ELIPHAZ TEXT	BILDAD TEXT
Fire burns up the wicked	15:30, 34	18:15
The prosperity of wicked ends	15:27-31	18:7, 15-16
Terror overtakes the wicked	15:21, 24	18:11, 14
Security of the tent of the wicked is removed	15:34	18:6. 14-15
The wicked do not know God	15:4, 13, 25-26	18:21
The wicked are caught in their own trap	5:13 (1st speech)	18:8-10

Just as Bildad began his first speech with the words: 'How long?' (8:2), so he again began his second speech in the same manner (18:2), as he tried to respond to Job's words in chapters 16 and 17.

To begin with, Bildad does not like the fact that Job had called him and his friends 'stupid beasts' (18:2-3; cf. 12:7-9). Bildad also tries to correct Job's declaration that it was 'God who had torn him in his anger' (16:9) by saying instead that it was no one less than Job himself who had torn himself apart in his own anger (18:4a). Anyway, Bildad continues, 'Who do you think you are, Job? Is God going to change the direction of nature just for your convenience?' (18:4b-c). Bildad apparently had reference to Job's earlier comment about the rocks being moved from their places (14:18). That would never happen, at least according to Bildad, so Job was just plain out of luck. Bildad was very hostile to Job and tired of his defenses for himself.

B. The wicked are destroyed – claims Bildad (18:5-21)
By referencing the lot of the 'wicked,' Bildad surely means this same response as his indirect answer to Job. First of all,

the 'lamp of the wicked is snuffed out' (18:5a), by which Bildad meant the prosperity and riches of the wicked would be extinguished. This was indeed meant to counter Job's earlier statement that 'the tents of the destroyers prosper' (12:6); however, Bildad has already countered one of Job's optimistic statements with his retort that 'the tent of the wicked will be no more' (8:22). He feels Job now stands corrected on the whole topic of the wicked! So there! Do you understand now, Job?

In verses 8-10, six synonymous words are used for a 'trap:' a 'net,' a 'mesh,' a 'trap,' (even a second Hebrew word for 'trap'), a 'snare,' a 'noose;' there are more references to a 'trap' in this text than in any other single Old Testament passage. By piling up these synonyms, Bildad is underscoring the dangers that lurked along life's road for the wicked, and presumably for Job too, if he would not confess (18:11). Bildad adds to Job's discomfort by saying that his troubles were about to eat him up, under the metaphor of 'his calamity is hungry' (18:12a), just as Job's skin problem in a like manner was also about to eat up his flesh (18:13).

This so-called 'comforter' announces that Job would be torn from his tent and marched off into captivity by the 'king of terrors' (18:14). Bildad has by now given Job a vivid description of what awaits him in the future, along with all the other wicked persons in death (15-21). The wicked would experience the fire and brimstone of God's judgment (18:15). They would be remembered no more (18:17), as they were banished into the outer darkness of death (18:18). Neither will his descendants survive his judgment (18:19), which would leave men and women everywhere gasping and thoroughly appalled (18:20). Bildad really lays it hard on Job, for to his way of thinking, when one realized that Job had lost his cattle, his children, his wealth, and his reputation, he too was indeed that same wicked person who was without God and without hope! The judgment of God surely indicated that very point! Wicked people suffer! Therefore, that is why Job was suffering, was it not?

2. Job's second reply to Bildad (19:1-29)

A. Job faces charges from the infamous trio (19:1-6)

Job begins his response by throwing back on his accuser, Bildad, his own introductory words in which he had questioned Job as follows: 'How long' would Job go on ranting and raving in his long-winded speeches?! If Bildad had twice begun his speeches with 'How long,' as he had, then Job too wanted to know 'How long' Bildad was going to 'torment' and 'crush' him as well (19:2). Job felt he had been insulted 'ten times' (19:3), a hyperbole meaning it 'had gone on for all too long now.' Moreover, even if Job had sinned, which accusation Job never once agreed to or admitted that he had, Job insisted that it still was none of their business; his own sin was his personal concern alone and that was that (19:4)! Actually, the three of them were, as a matter of fact, way off the mark in their condemnations of Job, for instead of his afflictions being indications or evidence that God was angry with Job, these purveyors of ancient 'fake news' had to know that it was God alone who had 'wronged' (the Hebrew actually has 'perverted') Job, according to Job's own view (19:5-6). All this was to counter Bildad's question: 'Does God pervert justice?' (8:3). Job had been trapped into making his own 'nets' or his own 'traps;' or so Bildad had claimed. But Job counters with a strong 'no,' it was God who had 'closed his net around' his servant Job (19:6b). Despite Bildad's use of six different words for 'traps' in 18:6-10, Job uses yet another word, meaning a 'hunter's net,' to trap animals when he too takes up the word. The three men were entrapping him in their own snares!

B. Job thinks God treats him as an enemy (19:7-12)
But of far more concern to Job than the charges of his false friends (19:6), was his feeling that God was the major force of hostility against him (19:7). The interesting point, however, is that both the accusing trio and Job all agreed that all Job's afflictions and sufferings were coming from God; nevertheless they disagreed on the reason for all these trials. The three men attributed this affliction to retribution for Job's sin, while Job attributed it to God's unfair treatment of him! That is why Job shouts out: 'I have been wronged!' (19:7a). Unfortunately, Job gets no immediate response from God and no immediate justice from heaven (19:7b), or an explanation. His complaint just hangs there in the thin air in front of his friends!

Job nevertheless continues to blame God for all his suffering. As Job evaluates the situation from all the evidence he has experienced, it all leads back to God as the ultimate source of his suffering. Here is a list of Job's complaints against God (8-12):

1. God has blocked my way by putting obstructions on my pathway. (8a)
2. God has overcast my path with darkness. (8b)
3. God has stripped me of my honor and reputation. (9a)
4. God has caused me a loss of esteem. (9b)
5. God has torn me down on every side until I was as good as dead. (10a)
6. God has uprooted my hopes like a tree is uprooted. (10b)
7. God's anger has burned against me. (11a)
8. God has treated me like an enemy. (11b)
9. God has besieged me like a city under attack. (12a)
10. God has encamped around my tent like an attacker. (12b).

Job raises up a pretty long list of accusations against God, but these were honest descriptions of how he felt. It might have helped Job had he known that it really had been God who all this time was the One who really was under examination and trial by Satan. It had been a wager that Satan had made, remember, as to whether Job trusted the Lord simply because God had been so good to him, or whether Job would trust God regardless of his circumstances? That had been Satan's attack on God, who was his first target, and his real focus was not primarily on Job! If only Job had known what was going on behind the scenes in heaven, it might have helped him a bit! But Job felt he was taking a hit from God, and he had no idea why or what it was all about!

C. Job describes his loneliness (19:13-22)

In addition to Job's loss of family, possessions, wealth, and reputation, he also was faced with the loss of his brothers, his acquaintances, his kinsmen, his friends, his guests, and his servants (13-16). Even his wife was offended by his bad breath and the little boys mocked and ridiculed him as well (17). How much more could Job take? This was turning out to be the worst time of his life!

Job felt he was totally cast out from all his former friendships and relationships. Those Job had loved in the past had now turned out to be against him (19). Physically, he was nothing but 'skin and bones;' he had escaped [or had such a close call on death that it was] only by the 'skin of his teeth'[2] that he had survived (20). As for the appearance of his body, he must have looked a mess!

Job pleaded with his friends: 'Have pity on me, my friends, have pity, for the hand of God has struck me' (21). But if God was afflicting him, Job's question was a pointed one to his visitors: 'Why do you pursue me [the same way] as God does?' (22). Job wanted to know why they continued to beat-up on him? Hadn't they had enough of using him as their theological football to toss around their single-track reason for suffering? Or what about this question: weren't they satisfied with the vengeance they had taken out on him as yet? Surely enough was enough, and Job had had his fill of all he could take from those who had formerly helped him and whom he had previously thought were his friends, but who actually had now turned-coat on

---

2. For the meaning of the phrase 'the skin of his teeth' see 'Dentistry and Teeth,' Edwin M. Yamauchi, (*Dictionary of Daily Life in Biblical and Post-Biblical Antiquity*, Hendrickson Publishers, Massachusetts, 2016).

him and become his enemies by accusing him of every sin they could think of.

D. Job remains confident that he will see his redeemer (19:23-29)

Roy Zuck called this chapter 19 the 'skyscraper among the forty-two chapters of Job that form the beautiful skyline of this poetic masterpiece.'[3] Here at the lowest emotional point in Job's series of trials, with the loss of all his family, his livestock, his wealth, his reputation, his friends, and his acquaintances, he suddenly cries out with a deep vibrant faith and a confident hope: 'I know that my Redeemer lives ... yet in my flesh I will see God' (19:25). Just when the blackest and darkest moment of his life have flooded over his consciousness, suddenly the sunlight of God's radiance breaks through to him in all of its splendor. It is at this point that we come to the best known portion of the whole book of Job, for here we have arrived at the peak of Job's confidence that he will not only personally be vindicated, but that he will be resurrected with his mortal body to be personally at home with his Advocate and heavenly Witness on high, i.e., indeed, with the Lord Himself.

Job begins this most magnificent outburst about his sure deliverance by requesting that his words would at least be 'recorded' and 'written on a scroll' (23). But as if that were not enough to preserve the permanence of what he wanted said about him, he asks in addition that his words would be chiseled deep into the rock with an

---

3. Zuck, p. 84.

'iron stylus' to engrave their message permanently into the hard surface of the stone. Then he further asks, in keeping with some of the known traditions of the Ancient Near East, that the dug-out and engraved letters carved into the stone also be filled with lead so there was very little chance that his words would ever be forgotten, chipped away, or blotted out by an enemy; whether it would be by time, by the ravages of the weather, or the work of an enemy (24). Thus the molten lead would fill the engravings in the rock as a future testimony for all to see just what his case consisted of.

But who then was this 'Redeemer' Job now appealed to? (25a). He is known as the 'Kinsman Redeemer,' (in Hebrew he was his *Go'el*), the One who would, for example, be his Advocate, who appeared in court to defend his cause in a lawsuit (Ps. 119:154; Prov. 23:11). The Kinsman Redeemer was also known at times to provide protection for a relative who could not defend himself or herself in life (Lev. 25:23-25; Ruth 4:4-15) and who would need someone who would avenge the fallen life of an unjustly or wickedly slain relative (Num. 35:19-27; 1 Kings 16:11). But even more importantly, this 'Redeemer' seemed to be parallel with the earlier 'Witness' mentioned in Job 16:19, who was 'in heaven' and 'on high' (16:19). How could this be a lesser figure than Messiah Himself, given His tasks and names?

Job had anticipated that his own death was perhaps about to happen soon, but he was just as certain that despite his upcoming death, his 'Defender' and 'Redeemer' would still rise up in the end to vindicate him, for he begins verse 25 with an emphatic stress on his own confidence with the words: 'I, even I.' Moreover, Job, not someone else, i.e., Job himself in his very own body, let it be noted, would one day look on his 'Redeemer' with his very own eyeballs – Job did not think this would be someone other than himself! (27). Job meant this: God would on a future day raise up Job from the grave right on this earth (literally, on 'the dust' from which mortals had been originally created) and be the One who had lived from all eternity, and who would live forever, the 'First' and the 'Last' (Isa. 44:60). Job would be able in that future day to see God in his very own person, in his very own flesh, and in his very own body. God would at that time be his 'Vindicator.' The point then was this: God would be Job's final 'Vindicator,' the One who would testify to Job's innocence and as a result, all would finally learn the truth about what Job had been going through all this time! That will be one glorious time indeed! Job would finally be vindicated by Messiah Himself!

The second half of verse 26 is just as important, for Job had said 'from [out of] my skin I shall see God.' Did he intend to say 'apart from my skin?' or did he mean 'from out of the vantage point of being from within my skin,' i.e., 'in my skin' I will see God? (for the Hebrew simply has the word 'from my skin'). Since he stressed he would see God with his own eyes, the reference is to the fact that Job in his own skin would look on God directly! This is the point Job also stressed in verse 27: 'I myself will see him with my own eyes – I and not another.' So overwhelmed was Job with this prospect of seeing God with his own eyeballs that: '[his] heart fainted within him' (27c).

So, to be clear on this matter, when did Job expect all of this to happen? Three options are presented to us; would it be: (1) after his death in his resurrected body, (2) in his lifetime before he died, or (3) somehow in his afterlife? Which was it?

Since he had said in verse 26a that this would be 'after [his] skin had been destroyed,' the first option is the preferred option here: it would be after his death, but Job would appear in a completely new resurrected body! This transformation could not be during his lifetime, for why then would he have needed his words to be left engraved in a rock and the carved-out letters filled with molten lead? Nor could it have been in a nebulous afterlife, where, according to some, there was no prospect of a resurrected body, for Job was going to see God again with his own eyeballs and right out of his own skin! What a grand prospect!

In the final two verses of this chapter, Job once again takes up the talk of his friends, who now wondered how they could hound him any further with a call to confess his sins, since Job himself contained the root of the problem they were concerned with (28)? But Job informs them that they had better watch out, because God's sword and punishment would come on their heads and not Job's head (29). This debate, it must be said, was not for sissies; it was a debate in earnest!

3. ZOPHAR'S SECOND AND FINAL SPEECH (20:1-29)

Zophar feels he has been personally attacked and that he has been dishonored by Job's remarks, which roused his anger mightily (20:1-2). But this third member of the Ash-Heap-Trio has nothing to say about Job's remarks about his expectation of being vindicated by his 'Redeemer.' Instead, he admits to being 'troubled' by what Job has said on other topics (20:2), but he still feels that his understanding forces him to answer the indomitable spirit of Job (20:3), who had previously asked what had caused both of them to answer Job in a trite and non-consequential way? (16:3).

Zophar cynically responds to Job with the remark that surely he was aware of the fact that ever since the first man (meaning Adam, of course), the celebration of the wicked was extraordinarily brief and their joy was but for the moment (20:4). Therefore Zophar concentrates in the rest of his speech in this chapter on the point that Eliphaz had raised already: the wealth of the wicked just will not endure; it will disappear – apparently just like Job's wealth had gone flying away (15:29).

With a move toward crassness, Zophar describes the meteoric rise of the wicked as reaching the heights of the heavens, so that their heady success touched the clouds, but such wicked persons would soon perish just like their own dung would disappear (20:6-7). Soon that same wicked man could no longer be found (20:8), for he would suddenly be banished from sight, just like the night would vanish. Whereas that same wicked man had been respected and highly regarded by others, once again, perhaps alluding to Job, suddenly he would no longer be seen (9). Moreover, that wicked man and/or his children would need to give back the wealth he/they had gathered dishonestly (10). Even the vigor that such a man had previously possessed would likewise die when he passed away (11). Zophar does not paint a very happy picture of the wicked. But even more significantly, it is clear by now that he means Job himself when he describes what is happening to the wicked.

Evil might be retained in the mouth of the wicked for a brief time, just like the flavor of sweets can be retained rather briefly in one's mouth, perhaps hidden under the tongue, as a person refuses to let the wonderful flavor leave his mouth, but that same taste of sweetness would turn to poison and act like the venom of a serpent, or at least, it would turn sour in his stomach (13-14), because of how that wealth had been obtained. Zophar was trying to say that sin may seem to be sweet for the moment, but the consequences were bitter indeed.

In the same way riches will need to be spat out when greed is allowed to accumulate heaps of riches that were gained unfairly and in an ill-gotten way (15). These gains will also need to be vomited out (15b). Holding on to such ill-gotten gains is like sucking the poison of serpents (16). Even the delicacy of the Near East, honey and curds (here used as symbols of the good life and easy prosperity)[4], must be yielded up because of the way they were gained (17-18). The wicked cannot get away with seizing what belongs to the poor and oppressing them in order to achieve personal success (19). Of course, by now Zophar has come to the conclusion that this must have been the way Job had become the wealthiest man in the Near East. This was the sin he had to confess to God if he was to be restored to health and wealth again.

---

4. See 'Insects.' and 'Milk and Milk Products,' Edwin M. Yamauchi, (*Dictionary of Daily Life in Biblical and Post-Biblical Antiquity,* Hendrickson Publishers, Massachusetts, 2016).

Such wicked crooks, Zophar lectures on, were driven by an insatiable greed (20); they just were unable to keep their hands off what others owned (21). However, just as this greedy, wealthy crook was arriving at the pinnacle of his success, distress would suddenly overtake him and he would know misery from then on (22). As he filled his belly with the goods that belonged to others, God Himself would rain down His blows on him (23). In fact, God would attack such a wicked man so fiercely that it would seem as if an army was after him all the way up to the day of his death (24-25). He might at first escape the iron weapon, but a bronze arrow would pierce him until he pulled it out of his liver (24-25). After this man's death, complete darkness would overwhelm his possessions and fire would devour what was left in his tent (26). Both the heavens and the earth would rise up against him as a flood would carry off his home (28). Zophar concludes with this final resounding blow, which was obviously aimed at Job. He says in effect: 'Sir, such is the fate God portions out to the wicked; this is God's appointed heritage for you!' (29). That was it: the gloves were now off and Zophar began to throw, as it were, body punches right at Job!

4. JOB'S SECOND REPLY TO ZOPHAR (21:1-34)

It seems as if Job waits until all three have spoken in the first cycle before he takes up as one their various emphases on retributive justice. Now, after the second cycle of speeches by the three visitors, Job picks up on the pervasive theme of this second batch of speeches offered by the three of them, which is how God destroys the wicked for their sin.[5] Thus,

---

5. This is the point made by Roy Zuck, ibid, p. 97.

Job calls for the visitors to 'listen carefully,' if they thought they were going to offer him any consolation (21:2). Zophar had been most aggressive in his attack on Job, so Job focuses more on him than on the other two.

Job directly opposes the claim of his supposed 'comforters,' for if they were correct about the fate of the wicked, then Job wants to know one thing: 'Why do the wicked live on, growing old and increasing in power?' (21:7). For example, much of Zophar's speech in chapter 20, Job outrightly rejects in chapter 21. A table of contrasts between the two men[6] would look like this:

Zophar's Claims – chapter 20	Job's Counterclaims-chapter 21
The joy of the wicked is brief – 20:5	The wicked live on – 21:7a
The wicked lose their loftiness – 20:6	The wicked become powerful – 21:7b
The wicked are forgotten when they die – 20:7-9	The wicked are given an honorable burial – 21:32-33
The wicked must beg from the poor – 20:10	The children of the wicked are happy – 21:12
The wicked perish like their own dung – 20:7	The wicked live – 21:7
The wicked do not suffer for their own sins – 20:10; 21:19	The wicked suffer for their own sins – 21:19-21.
The wicked lose their riches out of their bellies and cannot enjoy ease or prosperity – 20:15, 17-18	The wicked spend their days in prosperity – 21:13
The wicked lose the wealth of their houses – 20:21, 23, 28	The wicked live safely in their houses and their herds increase – 21:9-10

---

6. Modelled after the list in Roy Zuck, ibid, p 98.

At point after point, Job decisively disagrees with Zophar. As Job sees things, the wicked are doing quite well even though they outrightly reject the Lord. Job concludes in Job 21:16a that '… their prosperity is not in their own hands,' which seems to mean that they are helped by God Himself! Job distances himself from such a conclusion in the end (16b), but for the moment it certainly seems as if Job has totally sided with the wicked.

Job argues steadfastly that the wicked, no matter how rich or how poor they are, eventually die for their own sins (21:17-26). Moreover, in response to Bildad's claim that 'the light of the wicked goes out' (18:5), Job's challenge to him and to the others is this: 'How often is the lamp of the wicked snuffed out … [or does] calamity come upon them'? (17). And to Zophar's claim that the wicked are 'like a dream that flies away, no more to be found,' Job counters with this question: 'How often are they like straw before the wind, like chaff swept away by a gale'? (21:18). And if these wretched 'comforters' thought that they were going to answer Job by declaring that the children of the wicked would suffer retribution, Job will not allow that response either as being an adequate one.

It is said, 'God stores up a man's punishment for his sons' (19a). But Job comes back with this rejoinder: 'Let [God] repay the man himself, so that he will know it' (19b). Job has had enough talk from his three so-called 'friends.' Therefore he adds: 'Can anyone teach knowledge to God, since he judges even the highest'? (22). Job's three friends, in his estimation, were self-righteously presuming they were able to teach God what He could or could not do!

But they were clearly out of bounds in thinking or acting in that manner.

Job's view is that all the wicked do not die at the peak of their prosperity, for that is true only of some (23a), but others pass away while they are in full health and vigor, yet all the while enjoying complete security and living at ease (23b). Many of the wicked's bodies were 'well nourished' and their bones were 'rich with marrow' (24). Job's point is that his friends should not try to assess the outcome of someone's life by their lifestyle in this life, or in their general health, their bank account, or how they appear outwardly. All mortals will eventually die and only God can be the final and accurate judge of a person and his or her life.

Job was fully aware what his friends were thinking: They were thinking that Job had sinned and thus deserved what he was getting. But if they wanted to see things accurately, they should inquire of some of the people who had traveled the world (29). These travelers would confirm Job's point of view: 'the evil man is spared from the day of calamity ... he is delivered from the day of wrath' (30). In fact, many a wicked person is seen over and over again persisting in his evil lifestyle. Anyway, 'Who denounces his conduct to his face? Who repays him for what he has done?' (31). These rascals not only are honored while they are living, they even receive honor after they die (32), as a huge throng gathers for their funeral! (33b-c)

Job concludes that his three friends have failed miserably not only to comfort him, but also to answer any of his questions about why he is suffering (34). Instead of supplying him with answers to his quests, they have given him a lot of talk that had no application to Job himself.

Conclusions

Bildad and Zophar had totally failed to comfort Job and to answer his questions. Despite all their talk, they might as well have remained as quiet as they had been for the first seven days. They had not only totally misjudged Job and his pattern of life before God, but they had only one solution for suffering and that was that all suffering is the result of sin; thus, confession was necessary if one was going to start back on the road to success and pleasure in the eyes of God. Job must have sinned badly somewhere in his life! But Job knew that was not the case, so their advice was not worth anything.

QUESTIONS FOR REFLECTION
AND DISCUSSION

1. How would you like to have friends, such as this Ash-Heap-Trio, visit you when you were seriously ill with these answers as to why all this was happening to you?

2. If Bildad was somewhat milder in his assessments of Job and his problems, why was Zophar so steamed up over Job's responses? Did his speeches have any merit to them?

3. Why do both Bildad and Zophar mimic the thought and words of Eliphaz so much? Couldn't they see that the argument was not advancing anywhere?

4. What do you think of Job's responses? Does he fail the Lord, truth and righteousness in any way you can see?

5. To what degree has the argument progressed at the point of this second round of speeches, or has it been stymied now? What do you find in this lesson that can be used for persons who need help with their pain and suffering?

The Third Cycle

Chapter 7:
Job 22:1–26:14

Eliphaz and Bildad challenge
Job further

(Job 22:1–26:14)

Now that the second round of debates has concluded, Job 22:1 marks the start of the third cycle in the discussions. In this third round, only Eliphaz and Bildad speak, for Zophar has, for some reason, dropped out of the discussions.

As usual, Eliphaz the Temanite will lead off the debate. In his first discourse, Eliphaz's speech was generally smooth and well-stated with carefully crafted sentences. Moreover, in the first round of speeches, this apparent leader of the Ash-Heap-Trio showed some small courtesies to Job, but as he moved into the second round, all of the former politeness was dropped. But even more dramatically, we note that with his third cycle of talks, he begins to hit Job with unusual condemnatory force, even though his tough words and questions are somewhat cloaked with a soft velvet glove, yet it does appear that a change has swept over Eliphaz as he begins to lose his cool, for he boldly levels charges against Job. Eliphaz now piles one accusation upon another, followed by even more fiery invectives as he adds falsely invented, contrived, and leveled fake-charges against Job.

1. ELIPHAZ: GOD DOES NOT NEED MORTALS TO ACCOMPLISH HIS PURPOSES (22:1-4)

Eliphaz now argues that God does not have a need for a man's intervention or for his help. Nor does God profit from a 'vigorous man' (22:2), or from man's wisdom, or from his righteousness (22:3). It must be that Eliphaz thought that for all of Job's defending of himself, it was in Job's mind an actual defense of God's honor and reputation. Eliphaz assumes that Job thinks that by defending himself, he is in effect really defending God's honor. But on this assumption, Eliphaz is wrong once again in leveling this charge against Job.

It is true that Job did not understand God's actions towards him, or the lack of any reprieves from God towards him, but he never held to any view other than the fact that God was righteous and holy. It is at this point, then, that Eliphaz pops his key question: 'Is it for your piety that [God] rebukes you and brings [such] charges against you?' (22:4). Once again Eliphaz has gotten it all wrong, for he thinks Job felt that God was punishing him unfairly! But Job never said that God was in-the-wrong or that He had been unjust! Had Job said that, he would have done exactly what Satan wanted him to do: i.e., to accuse and blaspheme God. But that never happened! It is true, of course, Job did question God as to why he was suffering, but never once did Job say, or conclude: 'Lord, you've been unjust! You have been acting unrighteously towards me!' Eliphaz is instead inventing 'fake news' about Job, for as far as Job was concerned, he had never uttered such words or charges.

But we pause for a moment to emphasize that this is a key teaching point: Satan wants God's children to blame the Lord and accuse Him of being unfair and unjust when they suffer. If the evil one can press such a complaint from our own lips, then we might be willing to give in to his schemes and wicked strategies; thus he, for the moment, will have won the battle. However, if we have succumbed to Satan's strategy and wrongly charged God with unfairness on our behalf, we need to turn back to our Lord and confess our sin and ask for His forgiveness and help so that we do not do so again. But, mind you, Job never took that route. He refused to blame or charge God with wrong-doing!

Since Job never yielded to any of Eliphaz's accusations, Eliphaz therefore took another tactic, He would invent a series of extreme and unsubstantiated charges against Job, for in his view Job had to be guilty of some sin, for if he was not guilty, then why was he suffering? Job just had to be guilty! Thus, there would be more false accusations against Job.

2. ELIPHAZ NOW ACCUSES JOB WITH A NUMBER OF FALSE SOCIAL CHARGES (22:5-11)

Eliphaz by now must be terribly angry and almost frustrated to death by Job's responses. Something was wrong, but he could not identify the problem! Instead, he fabricates a whole list of social crimes that a man of his position, with his power and influence, must have meted out at one time or another on his compatriots. Eliphaz begins by seeking to intimidate and charge Job with questions like: 'Is not your wickedness great? Are not your sins endless?

[Haven't] you stripped men of their clothing, leaving them naked?' (5-6). Eliphaz would have known that in his day this was a sin. It is what perhaps later appeared in the law of Moses, which had warned mortals that forcing a man to hand over his outer garment to a creditor as a pledge for a payment, yet without returning it to him for protection from the cold of the night, was a violation of what God had taught (Exod. 22:26-27; Deut. 24:10-13). To this charge, however, Job would later respond directly with a solid denial (Job 31:19-22).

But Eliphaz is not finished, for he is just warming to his subject. He charges Job with giving 'no water to the weary and … withhold[ing] food from the hungry' (22:7). But this too was a trumped-up accusation, for Job also put this charge to rest later on in Job 31:17-22, just as he had handled similar false charges against him.

Eliphaz is now on a roll, for he levels a third invented misdeed against Job in 22:9. He charges Job with abusing the rights and the protection he and all others owed to widows and orphans, even though Job was 'a powerful man, owning land – an honored man, living on [the land].' But such a social blunder was an outrageous sin, for the Lord takes special notice and care of widows and orphans; how then could Job, or any other mortal, do less than his Lord exhibited? Job denied this charge as well!

3. ELIPHAZ FURTHER ACCUSES JOB OF DEFYING GOD (22:12-20)

As if it were not offensive enough to invent such sins against a brother, Eliphaz goes on to invent even more false charges against him. Now Eliphaz decides to twist what Job has said and make him say something he has not said at all. Eliphaz: 'Job, your trouble is that you think God is up in the heights of heaven, therefore, he doesn't see all the sins you commit!' (22:12-13). But that too was blatantly wrong. Job knew that everything was open to the gaze of God. Job never would have had a desire to ask: 'What does God know [about me]?' (13a). 'Can [God] judge through the thick darkness?' (13b). Can even the 'thick clouds veil him so he does not see us, as [God] goes about in the vaulted heavens?' (14). Surely Eliphaz has just heard Job affirm in 21:22 the fact that God was omniscient and that, as God, He saw everything. Eliphaz has nevertheless deliberately misconstrued Job's words. Even worse, he asks mockingly, 'Will you keep to the old path that evil men have trod?' (15), men who 'were carried off before their time, their foundations washed away by a flood?' (16). This so-called 'friend' mocked Job like a little child would mock another person by repeating their words back to them in a bratty, perhaps even in a sing-song fashion. By alluding to the flood of Noah's day, Eliphaz places Job in the crowd of wicked people of Noah's day. Eliphaz continues to play with Job's words from Job 21:14-16 as he deliberately distorts them in 22:17-18 as this miserable comforter continues to give Job's words a double meaning.

4. Eliphaz once again appeals to Job to repent (22:21-30)

There just could not have been a more elegant appeal for Job to repent, for Eliphaz, in verses 21-23, gives a most urgent call for Job to admit his sin and turn to God. He urges Job to:

'Submit to God,' 'be at peace with him,' 'accept instruction from his mouth,' 'Lay up [the Lord's] words in your heart,' 'return to the Almighty,' remove wickedness from your heart,' and 'assign your nuggets to the dust, your gold of Ophir[1] to the rocks in the ravines.' If Job would do these things, then 'in [that] way, prosperity [would] come to him' (21b).

Furthermore, if Job would do these things, then 'the Almighty would be [his] gold' and he would 'find [much] delight in the Almighty' (26); 'light would shine on [his] ways' (28b), and all he would decide to do '[would] be done' (28a). '[God] [would] save the downcast' (29b).

5. JOB REPLIES TO ELIPHAZ (23:1–24:25)

Eliphaz's diatribe had, no doubt, really hit Job hard, for it seemed as if his frustration and loneliness rises to a new level as he responds to Eliphaz's attack. Job's call to God becomes even more acute as he summarizes it all in two key problems: (1) the injustice of his own case (23:1-7), and (2) the injustices in the world (23:8-17). But what irks Job the most is that the evil perpetrated by the wicked seems to escape any punishment (24:1-25).

A. Job longs once again for God to hear his case (23:1-12)
Here is Job's constant wish: if only he could locate where the Lord was, he would go to His dwelling and state his case (3-4). Then Job would know directly from the Lord

---

1. The third argument supporting a a later dating of the book of Job concerns the references (also on p. 160) to 'the gold of Ophir.' Wherever Ophir was, its gold would not have been known prior to Solomon's importation of it. See Edwin M. Yamauchi, *Africa and the Bible*, (Baker Academic, Grand Rapids, Michigan, 2009), pp. 82-91.

what answers God would give to him (5). But God was, as a matter of fact, elusive, if He was not indeed hidden. Job did not think that God might oppose him 'with [his] great power' (6a) but there was one thing he was certain of: God 'would not press charges against him,' for his life was clean (6b). God was so fair and so equitable that 'an upright man could present his case before him, [and he] would be delivered forever by [this] judge' (7). Thus, Job would act as his own attorney and he would present his case as persuasively as possible before God's court (4). Certainly, Job thought he could count on God's response to be more comforting and sensitive than the case being made so far by the Ash-Heap-Trio! Job would pay attention to what God said to him, but as for his false 'friends,' they were far from the mark of truth as they related to him, or far from being of any help to him anyway.

But if God is to hear Job's case, He must first be found. So, Job looks to the east, then to the west, to the north, and to the south, but he never even catches a glimpse of him (8-9). Nevertheless, despite the fact that God remains elusive to Job, Job is certain that God none-the-less knows about him (10). And that when God will finally appear in court with Job, he is sure that he will be found innocent as he would come forth as pure as gold (10b). The reason Job is so certain he would emerge from God's court as an innocent man is due to the fact that '[he has] kept to [God's] way without turning aside' (11b), nor has he 'departed from the commands of [God's] lips' (12a). In fact, Job asserts that he has 'treasured the words [out] of [God's] mouth more than [his own] daily bread' (12b).

B. Job recoils a little from the thought of standing alone before God (23:13-17)

Eliphaz and his buddies were wrong, of course, to keep insisting that if Job would only repent, his life and plans would be different (22:28). Instead, Job knew that the Lord had a plan for his life and God was in the act of carrying it out (23:14). However, God was so mysterious and unique in who He was and how He did things that Job was often filled with a sense of terror and faint-heartedness at the prospect of standing before Him (23:14-15). But that was not the bottom line for Job, for in spite of the darkness and the gloom, Job would not be silenced in the least in his quest to appear before God (23:17).

C. Job complains that God does not punish those who deserve it (24:1-25)

Job begins his complaint by asking: 'Why does the Almighty not set times for judgment, [so that] ... those who know him [do not] look in vain for such days?' (24:1). This was a question that did not seem to fit Job's view of God, for had he not just said that God 'stood alone' and did 'whatever he pleased' (23:13)?

i) Job: Why is God apparently so apathetic toward judging the wicked? (24:2-17)

Job lists three sins the wicked practice: (1) moving the boundary stone, (2) stealing someone else's flocks, and (3) mistreating the needy by driving off the donkeys that orphans were caring for, or taking the widow's ox in pledge (24:2-4). As a result of these wicked abuses, these victims had to hunt for food in the desert like wild donkeys, pick up fodder in the fields, glean the vineyards of the wicked, and sleep with no protective clothing to shield them from the cold nights, while being exposed to the drenching rains that soaked them as they stayed close to the rocks to gain as much shelter as they could (24:5-8). Even more vile were the acts of those who stole fatherless babies from their mothers, even while the baby was being nursed. To add to this, they seized the clothing of the poor, leaving them naked and hungry (24:9-10). Job's list goes on: for the wicked forced the poor to carry sheaves, to crush olives into oil, and tread the winepresses while experiencing great hunger and thirst themselves (24:10b-11). Job laments the fact that so far God has not charged anyone with wrong doing (24:12c)! Surely God sees what is going on; why then does He appear to be so oblivious to the deeds of the wicked? Would judgment never come to these oppressors?

If God sees all of this wrongdoing, why, then, was He holding back His hand of judgment? (24:17). These murderers, adulterers, and housebreakers rebelled against the light of God's Word and continued to do their work in the darkness of night (24:13-17).

ii) Job: Still confident that the wicked would get what was coming to them (24:18-25)

The change in the direction of Job's speech is so sudden, that some think that verses 18-25 contradicts what Job has just said. But Job does now assert that God will, as a matter of fact, punish the wicked. For Job declares that those oppressors he had just listed in the previous section of 24:1-17 were in fact no more substantial, or the determiners as to how history would end, than foam on the surface of the water (24:18a). Moreover, their land was cursed, and their vineyards were not worth any further attention (24:18b-c). The wicked would perish in Sheol (=the grave) in the same way that snow melts in a drought and then evaporates (24:19). Such evil persons would be forgotten by the wombs of those that bore them, and the only ones remembering them would be the worms that feasted on them. Their wickedness would be cut off suddenly, much like a tree that is felled (24:20).

Those evil persons who preyed on the barren and childless widows would be dragged off by God when He judged them, for they would have no assurance of life (24:21-22). It might for the moment seem as if God had forgotten about the wicked, but 'his eyes were on their ways' (24:23). It would not make any difference to God's judgment of their station in life, whether they were high in rank, great in wealth, or mighty in influence; they would be 'cut off like heads of grain' (24:24). Job concludes his response to Eliphaz by challenging the 'Ash-Heap-Trio' to prove him wrong and show him and all others that his words amounted to nothing (24:25).

6. Bildad extols God's greatness and sees man as a maggot or a worm (25:1-6)

Bildad the Shuhite poses this rhetorical question: 'How then can a man be righteous before God?' (25:4a), which is a repetition of the question Eliphaz began with in his vision in 4:17a. But Job had also posed the identical question in 9:2b. To this question, Bildad continued to ask, just as Eliphaz had: 'How can one born of woman be pure?' (25:4b). This too, as we noted, was an echo of some of Eliphaz's earlier inquiries in 4:17b; 15:14). So why was Bildad just going over the same ground and themes that had been played out previously with no obvious help to Job? Did Bildad think that Job would finally realize that he too was included in what was said about the whole human race? Of course, what Bildad said about God in 25:2 was true, but his problem was that he, along with his two friends, continued to cling to the false premise that Job was suffering because of some hidden sin in his life. That, once more, just was not so!

Therefore, in order to place Job in his proper place, Bildad declares that 'Dominion and awe belong to God; he [alone] establishes order in the heights of heaven' (25:2). God as Creator has a majesty and magnificence that exceed all other parts of the created order He has made. For example, Bildad points to the moon and the stars, though made by God, they still are not as bright as God is in all His splendor.

But Job would not have objected to any of those statements about the majesty of God. Bildad adds that the moon and stars were 'not pure in [God's eyes]' (25:5b). That must have been a remark to set up Job, for Bildad immediately notes 'how much less man' (25:6; here Bildad used the word for 'man,' meaning a 'weak man'). 'Man is but a maggot,' Bildad argues (25:6a), which must have been another attempt to cut Job down a peg or two. Bildad was sick of Job claiming he was innocent of all the charges the three 'comforters' had brought against him. Bildad wanted Job to face up to his own worthlessness – Job was 'only a worm.' (25:6b); which worms were just as 'weak' as Job was. The Scriptures report that Bildad said this, but the Lord never made such a statement anywhere in Scripture about any mortal. Instead, God viewed humans as being valuable and made in His image. They were never treated as 'maggots' or 'worms,' even when they went deep into sin's grip. People were not worms or maggots, but they were very valuable in the eyes of the Almighty, so Bildad had it all wrong! Mortals were just not a heap of junk!

However, despite Bildad's brief attempts to challenge Job, his speech was fruitless and utterly hopeless without any comfort to a man racked by pain and suffering. With this as the final word from the 'Ash-Heap-Trio,' the collected words of Job's three friends mercifully come to an end. Good riddance to the three of them, for they were of little, if any, help!

7. Job answers Bildad with irony (26:1-14)
A. Job's response to Bildad (26:1-4)
Even though this chapter is part of Job's longest speech, extending from chapter 26 to 31, it is best to view chapter 26 as a reply to Bildad since the pronoun 'you' is in the singular form in 26:2-4, but 'you' in 27:5 now appears

in the plural form and thus constitutes Job's grand finale, and concluding speech, to all three of the Ash-Heap-Trio. Therefore, we shall treat chapter 26 by itself and note that it has two parts: (1) Job's response to Bildad (26:1-4), and (2) Job's own statement on the greatness of God. When compared to the statement of the same theme by Bildad, Job's statement about God is exceedingly more descriptive and glorifying to God (26:5-14).

Job could not begin on a more sarcastic note as he decries Bildad's weak attempt to intimidate him; his words drip with sarcasm and irony:

> 'How you have helped the powerless! How you have saved the arm that is feeble! What advice you have offered to one without wisdom! And what great insight you have displayed! Who has helped you utter these words? And whose spirit spoke from your mouth?' (26:2-4).

If Bildad thought Job was all that 'weak' and short on strength and wisdom, how had this 'comforter' helped him or given him any hope and quietude? Anyway, who in the world had helped Bildad to conjure up such an assortment of words? They must have been words from his own mind and ones of his own invention, for they certainly were worth zero as far as Job was concerned. One thing for sure, they certainly were not inspired words from God, for Bildad's assumptions about Job's guilt were way off base! Job had had enough of these 'miserable comforters,' for their minds were made up and there was no use trying to talk to them any longer.

B. Job returns to the theme of the greatness of God (26:5-14)
Job had stressed the theme of the Greatness of God on several occasions in his previous rebuttals: Job 9:4-10; 12:13-25, and now he returns to this same theme once again in 26:5-14. Job, however, must have been deeply wounded and hurt by Bildad's parting jab against him – that he belonged to the order of the 'worm' and 'maggot' (25:6). Thus, whereas Bildad and Zophar had stressed the ultimate fate of the sinner, while saying very little about the magnificence or the majesty of God, Job had constantly taken refuge in that thought. In this text, Job will lay down the facets of the majesty of God in His creation and in His being.

Job begins by alluding to the 'dead' (Hebrew, *harepha'im*)[2], apparently meaning the elite dead, who trembled in the face of the majesty of God, even though the dead were in 'Abaddon' (26:5-6). *Abaddon* appears a mere six times in the Old Testament[3] as the place where the dead lived. This may have been the same place that was 'beneath the waters' (26:5).

Job goes on to magnify God's work of creation by likening it to God's act of spreading out the skies, just as one would put up and spread out a tent. The earth, however, our Lord 'suspended [or hung] over nothing' (7b).

---

2. The word 'Rephaim' appears in Ugaritic meaning 'giants' as well as a reference to chief gods. It appears in Ps. 88:10; Prov. 2:18; 9:18; 21:16; Isa. 14:9; 26:14, 19. Roy Zuck, *Job*, p. 117, n 6 cites Conrad L'Heureux, 'The Ugaritic and Biblical Rephaim,' *Harvard Theological Review* 67 (1974):265-74.

3. As noted by Roy Zuck, *Job*, p. 117, n 7. The six places where this word occurs are: Job 26:6; 28:22; 31:12; Ps. 88:11, margin, Prov. 15:11; 27:20.

This was a thought that must have shocked the Ash-Heap-Trio and all who have read it subsequently. Who but God would know this fact as well? The clouds God made to 'wrap up the waters [in the sky],' … 'yet the clouds do not burst under their weight' (8). Moreover, our Lord used the clouds to 'cover the face of the full moon' (9). Job then moves on to magnify God's work in setting boundaries on the waters covering the earth, as the horizon also marked the distinction between light and darkness (10).

By 'the pillars of heaven,' Job refers to the mountains that God had made (11). And even though these pillars were also strong, they too trembled, quaked (or He 'restrained' them), and stood 'aghast at [the Lord's] rebuke' (12). What is more, by the power of God, He 'churned up' (or: 'restrained') the sea, as the Lord 'cut Rahab in pieces' (12b; Rahab was a name for the sea god or 'fleeing/gliding serpent,' perhaps equated to 'Leviathan in Isa. 27:11). Moreover, the Lord made the skies clear by the breath of His mouth and His hand 'pierced the gliding serpent' (13).

What a superb description of the power and majesty of God at work in creation! Even with such details we are given here, claims Job, we only have 'the outer fringes of [God's] works' (14a). Job's wretched comforters had tried with their words to intimidate and to terrify Job by describing God's power and might, but Job has an even more pronounced and distinguished view of the greatness and magnificence of God. God manifested Himself in the realm of the dead, in the skies and clouds, and in the beauty of the sea. So, their attempt to scare Job fell flat! Job rejoiced in the majesty and greatness of God!

CONCLUSIONS

1. The key question remains the same for all involved in this discussion: 'Can a mortal man be more righteous before God?'

2. But Job still wants to appear before God, so he can hear what He has to say about all that he is experiencing. Surely God knows that Job has done nothing wrong to deserve all of this. Interestingly enough, we his readers know precisely what Job did not know about what was going on here behind the scenes in heaven. He was indeed innocent.

3. Job declared that he treasured God's words more than his daily bread.

4. But Job could not understand why God seemed to be slow to move in judgment against the wicked.

5. Job defied anyone to prove him false and to reduce his words to nothing. He claimed he was innocent before God.

6. God was so magnificent that few if any could understand the thunder of His power.

QUESTIONS FOR REFLECTION
AND DISCUSSION

1. How was it possible for Eliphaz and Bildad to say so many things that were correct about God and yet be so wrong when it came to applying them to Job? Are we today better at interpreting Scriptures than we are in applying them?

2. Why were Eliphaz and Bildad trying to frighten and intimidate Job with the greatness and majesty of God? Did this strategy make sense?

3. How did Job get the information that God hung the earth on nothing? How did that anticipate modern science?

4. Did Eliphaz's speech sound similar to the message of a prosperity, health, and wealth preacher, or was he making another point that had validity?

5. If Eliphaz and Bildad were correct in asking 'How can a man be righteous before God?' why do we discount what they had to say in this context about Job?

6. Is it proper for a believer to use irony and sarcasm to answer those who are doubtful of the proper application of the Word of God to their unbelieving circumstances?

Chapter 8:
Job 27:1–31:40

Job mightily asserts his innocence once and for all

'I will maintain my righteousness and never let go of it; my conscience will not reproach me as long as I live' (Job 27:6).

In these five chapters,[1] Job begins an especially strong defense of his life and walk with God. Consequently, he begins what we might call, as Martin Luther declared, his 'Here I stand [Speech], I can do no less.' Job takes a strong stand with an assertion that he would stand firm in his claim all the way to the end, as he set forth his case in this manner:

> As surely as God lives, who has denied me justice, the Almighty, who has made me taste bitterness of soul, as long as I have life within me, the breath of God in my nostrils, my lips will not speak wickedness, and my tongue will utter no deceit. I will never admit you [so-called 'comforters'] are in the right; till I die, I will not deny my integrity. I will maintain my righteousness and

---

1. Some commentators think they see a muddled order in chapters 26-27 with parts of each chapter being allocated to Bildad and Zophar. But we find that they both belong to Job as he makes one angry outburst against his three friends starting in chapter 27 and continuing on into chapter 31, with a brief respite in chapter 28.

> never let go of it; my conscience will not reproach me as
> long as I live.' (27:2-6).

This is where Job has begun to take his stand and where he will continue to maintain his innocence until the day he dies. Come what may, his mind has been made up and he will not concede an inch.

1. JOB TAKES HIS STAND PRIMARILY ON THE WORD OF GOD (27:1-23)

With this statement, Job throws down the gauntlet to his three testy visitors. He makes it clear that he would never admit that they were in the right and he would never deny his own integrity. In many ways, Job's determination to stick with his claim of innocence is reminiscent of another historic moment that took place at the Cathedral in Worms, Germany, where Dr. Martin Luther was summoned before the heads of the Holy Roman Empire on October 31, A.D. 1517. On that occasion, all the leaders of the Roman Catholic Church, and many of the nobles of the empire, were present to hear what Luther would answer to the charges of theological heresy leveled against him. As Luther fought to stand his ground, he famously answered the charges against him by saying:

> Unless I am shown by the testimony of Scripture and
> by evident reasoning, unless I am overcome by means of
> the Scriptural passages that I have cited, and unless my
> conscience[2] is taken captive by the words of God, I am

---

2. Conscience must be taken captive by the Word of God, as Luther so correctly put it. It must therefore be trained, but it must not be ignored if the Lord Jesus has become our conscience. See David Atkinson, *The Message of Job: Suffering and Grace,* (Downers Grove, IL, InterVarsity Press, 1991), p. 104.

neither able nor willing to revoke anything, since to act against one's conscience is neither safe nor honest. Here I stand; God help me, I cannot do otherwise, Amen.

But there is a difference between Luther's famous stance and Job's courageous defense before his three 'comforters': Luther was defending the Word of God, but Job insisted on defending himself and his own reputation, just as Ray Steadman observed. Job would defend his innocence to his dying breath. He would maintain his righteousness and never let go of it (6). These claims of his innocence are not new, of course, but they are consistent with his stance all along, for this is how he had responded not only to Eliphaz (6:10, 29-30; 16:17; 23:10-12), but also to Bildad (9:35; 10:7), and to Zophar (12:4; 13:18-19). Job had never denied that the wicked eventually would be punished; he only questioned why the wicked continued to prosper and to be at ease for so long a time, apparently without God intervening to put an end to them and their foolish deeds of wickedness.

Job now calls his three friends his 'enemies' (7). Moreover, Job turns the arguments of his three visitors back on their own heads, for according to their own words, if any had falsely accused another, which in this case would have been Job against himself, then those liars were the ones who would be punished under the law of Israel. Thus, if all they had said about the punishments coming to the wicked for the wicked doing such things as rendering a false testimony, which of course the Ash-Heap-Trio had wrongly aimed at Job, these three 'comforters' were themselves in deep trouble; and Job had since cleared his name in the meantime of all such crimes they had invented against him. Moreover, what the three of them had said about the children of these wicked persons would instead happen to their own children – they would be killed by the sword (14-15); it was their wealth that would all disappear in a day (16-23); it was they who would go to bed rich, but wake up destitute and poor (19). Terrors would flood over them and suddenly destroy them (20). Even the house of the wicked would be as shaky and unstable as the cocoon of a moth, or the hut of a watchman (18). All of this began as Job uttered the absolute reliability of his words by taking an oath: 'As surely as God lives' (2a), which showed thereby that all Job was going to claim, would be as sure and certain as the very existence of God Himself!

2. JOB SHOWS MANKIND'S INABILITY TO DISCOVER GOD'S WISDOM (28:1-28)

Many regard this chapter 28 as one of the most beautiful passages in the whole book of Job, for now in this interlude, which follows the hard dialogue between Job and his three so-called 'friends,' is a break from the intensity and the hard give-and-take of this debate. The four men must have felt exhausted from the hard trading of words back and forth to each other – as we the readers likewise feel exhausted by now just from reading this account! They needed a break and so do we! Job therefore pauses to meditate on the persistent search for wisdom and understanding on such matters as his suffering and pain.

This chapter also has special relevance for Job's three counselors, for they had presumed to know the ways of God fully. But Job counters their stubborn assertions with the fact that humankind is not always able to discern the wisdom of God, especially if it involves the inscrutable mysteries of such a majestic God as he worships. Hence a breathing space is now provided in chapter 28 as we are given a marvelous discussion and a beautiful Hymn to Wisdom, one of God's beautiful gifts!

A. The quest for wisdom is way beyond the search for metals and jewels (28:1-11)
Job begins by admiring the skill of the miners who dig for treasures in the earth. As such, these miners knew where a mine for silver existed, or the place where gold could be found (1). 'But where [on earth] could wisdom be found?' [That was the hardest question of all]. 'Where does understanding dwell?' [that too was another tough question] (12). If all the dialogue thus far illustrated anything, it simply was the fact that wisdom was more elusive than the search for any of the precious metals or jewels of the rarest form.

Job begins by describing mining practices that he knew of in his day, which amazingly seemed to show that not much about mining[3] has changed all that significantly from Job's day until ours. True, mortals needed light in order to search for silver, gold, iron, copper in the dark and remote recesses of the underground mine. It was also true

---

3. See 'Mining.' Edwin M. Yamauchi, *Dictionary of Daily Life in Biblical and Post-Biblical Antiquity,* (Hendrickson Publishers, Massachusetts, 2016).

that miners in Job's day cut a shaft inside the mountain, or a hole in the earth, and then braced up the sides of the shaft with scaffolding as they burrowed deeper into the mountain side, or into the earth in search of these metals and jewels. These men risked their lives to reach these objectives, where no animal or bird even dared to go, nor whose skill matched the miner's skill (7-8). Human beings, it seemed, would do almost anything to assault the flinty rocks, or tunnel deep down into the heart of a mountain or into the deep recesses of the earth in their search to bring these riches to the light of day (9-11). But that was not the same as finding wisdom!

But when men search for wisdom itself, they take on a job that is exceedingly more difficult than that of any mining operation described here (12, 20). How was wisdom to be found and where should we go to locate it?

B. Wisdom is the hardest treasure to find (28:12-19)

Job, however, sought for wisdom, just as intensively as other men sought for precious metals and costly stones. Wisdom, of course, was a much more valuable item than these rare metals and stones (13). If one tried to locate wisdom in the depth of the sea, the sea would declare 'It is not with me.' Even if someone wanted to purchase wisdom, such wisdom could not be purchased with the finest of gold, for example, for not even the price for the gold of Ophir, or that paid for with precious onyx or sapphire gems (15-16) could compensate for its worth and value. The price of wisdom was exceedingly more costly, even than the price of rubies (18b). Wisdom was simply priced out of the market for mortals, for it was not easily obtained, even if one were rich in wealth and great possessions. It just could not be bought for any amount, for its value was beyond all precious metals or exquisite jewels. Anyway, it just wasn't for sale! True wisdom was not of this world, 'it [was] hidden from the eyes of every living thing' (21).

C. Wisdom can only be found in the Lord (28:20-28)
Verse 23 begins in the Hebrew text by placing God's name (Hebrew, *Elohim*) first, and thereby emphasizing the importance of the name of God in the search for a solution to the problem of where wisdom could be found or obtained. God alone knew where wisdom dwelt (23b), for the Lord alone could see to the ends of the earth – in fact, He could see everything under all the heavens (24). Thus, when God set the velocity for the wind on earth and measured out the amount of water the earth was to receive, He made a decree for the patterns of rain, and the course of the thunderstorm. In the same way He simultaneously looked at wisdom as He confirmed and tested it. It was at that time that God said, 'The fear of the Lord – that is wisdom, and to shun evil is understanding.' (28). Therefore, until human beings learn to fear the Lord and to shun evil, they will be markedly deficient in wisdom. Our Lord perfectly understood and established wisdom, just as He established the regulations and functions of nature by His creative hand. It is also clear that there are two aspects to obtaining wisdom: the principle of the fear of Adonai and the warning 'to depart from evil.' Thus, while mortals are unable to purchase or to discover wisdom, yet it is possible to know wisdom, for it is the Lord Himself

who can and will unveil to mortals what otherwise would remain 'hidden from the eyes of all living' (28:21) unless we came to Him first of all.

Job 28 fits in nicely with God's earlier assessment of Job (1:1, 8; 2:3). But this chapter is also a rebuke to Job's three friends for their myopic and limited view of God. Whereas Job has shown wisdom at its best by fearing God and by steering away from evil, it was not clear that his three friends had done the same. Seen in this light, Job 28:28 with its double injunction to fear God and to shun evil marks a high-water mark in the book of Job! But this final statement also serves as a great transition to Job 29-31.

It is in Job 29 that Job lists examples of his virtue in the past as evidence that he, as a matter of fact, did indeed fear God and shun evil. But in Job 31 he shows how he, in case after case, turned away from evil, even in its smallest forms, and thus was fully innocent of the made-up charges that the Ash-Heap-Trio was incorrectly charging him with.

3. Job yearns for the immediacy of God's presence (29:1-25)

In a wistful way, Job wishes he could go back again to those earlier days and months – now gone (29:1-2). Apparently, this reference to 'months' indicates that several months of suffering his pains have now gone by since this disaster had overtaken him. During those former days, Job reminisced, he had been able to walk through many of those difficult times with the lamp of God shining on his way (3). Then it was that 'the Almighty was still with [him]' and '[his] children were [still] around [him]' (5). He had been unusually prosperous as 'cream/butter'[4] and 'streams of olive oil' poured out of the land and rocks benefitting him (6). He also enjoyed high social regard as he sat with the elders at the city gate to judge public affairs when needed (7-11). Job was respected by both the young men and the old men (8). So sought after was his counsel that nobles, princes, and persons of rank in the community waited in deference to him to hear his wisdom and his advice on the matters raised in the gate (9-11). Moreover, because he took up the cause of the poor and others such as the orphans and the oppressed, God blessed him and gave him good judgment, words of wisdom, and deep respect from the community (29:12-20). In fact, his careful use of the gift of justice was so characteristic of his style and decorum that they were like his robe and like a turban on his head (14). Any who were lame, blind, or similarly handicapped, he specially cared for as if he were their father (15-16). Whenever someone was about to devour an injured or hurting person, Job acted by snatching them from the fangs of the oppressors and defended them in the cause of justice (17).

Job had thought he would die in his own home with a full lifetime of experiencing the blessings and approval from God as he enjoyed strength every day from God and a respected regard, and a high estimation, from all who knew him (18-20). Each time Job spoke, men would wait for his counsel in silence (21-23). What Job

---

4. Ibid., see 'Milk and Milk Products.'

said satisfied these citizens, for they drank in everything he had to say (23). Even the expression on Job's face showed his gracious deportment of giving comfort to his fellow mortals, rather than a scolding word of condemnation (24). Job's ministry also included comforting all those who grieved (25).

4. JOB CONTRASTS 'THEN' WITH WHAT HE EXPERIENCES 'NOW' (30:1-31)

A. How the low-life who had so little now mocked and scorned Job (30:1-15)

Things have changed drastically and horribly since the wonderful days that Job has just finished recalling in chapter 29, for Job would now describe his present situation in 30:1, 9, and 16 with those world-changing-words: 'But now.' Whereas Job had been deeply respected in the past, now men who were younger than Job, and whose fathers he would not even put in charge of his sheep dogs, freely and viciously mocked him (30:1).

Job was acutely aware of how far he had been removed from those good old days, when he was walking with the Lord and was experiencing God's blessing and prosperity. Now, at least some of those he had helped in the past, were instead making fun of him (1). Usually those who were elders were accorded deep respect in the Ancient Near East, but now Job has been reduced by his suffering and economic disasters so that those who were much younger than he, heaped scorn and ridicule on him. But these scallywags were just plain weak and useless (2). These same tramps bore the marks of famine and hunger as they roamed the parched land in their efforts to get food (3). Their food came from the sour tasting leaves of the broom-shrub that grew in the marshes (4). These same snobs were banished from society and were treated as if they had been thieves (5). Their homes were in caves and dry wadis (6) as they huddled together under thorn bushes and brayed like wild donkeys and acted as fools who were expelled from the land (7-8).

The fathers' children mocked Job perhaps in a sing-song manner, as Job became no more than a byword among them (9). These kids mostly kept their distance from Job, and yet at times would not even hesitate to spit in his face (10). Since these ruffians saw Job as being afflicted by God, they felt no compunction about unleashing any kind of attacks on him (11). In addition to the verbal assaults Job had to bear from this 'brood' of turncoats, they also insisted on attacking him physically as they laid snares for his feet and broke up the path ahead of him (12-14). Job felt terrorized and overwhelmed as he suffered the loss of his dignity and his safety vanished (15).

B. How Job felt disregarded by God (30:16-23)

Ultimately, however, Job felt most abandoned by God, for he attributed the physical and emotional suffering he was feeling to God. It was as if his very life was ebbing away and his zest for living was gone (16). Even in the night, when one might expect to find some relief, Job felt no respite (17). In fact, Job describes God as the one who tightly gripped his neck as the color of his robe gripped him in like manner (18)! Moreover, God further treated him roughly by throwing him into the mud and reduced him to ashes and dust (19), or he thought it was so! Job claims he had cried out to God, but God did not answer (20). No longer did Job regard God as being passively indifferent; here he depicted the Sovereign of the universe as being a ferocious animal (21) or like a mighty storm (22) attacking him. The end of all this divine activity would conclude, Job argued, with his death, ending 'the house of all living' (23b).

C. How Job was neglected by mortals as well (30:24-31)
Job insists he has been treated unfairly by many, for when others have cried out for help in their distress, at least no one laid a hand on them. But in my case, Job laments, I have not been treated that way. Despite the fact that in my lifetime, I have wept and grieved for the poor, yet when it came my turn for some sympathy, I got no respect; instead I got evil and insults (24-26). Even Job's Ash-Heap-Trio failed to offer him any comfort or solace.

Job relates how he was emotionally in constant turmoil and without any comfort (27-28). He apparently burned with fever (30) constantly. His harp and flute, the instruments that normally were his output of joy and happiness, were now tuned only to funeral dirges as people poured out their grief (31). Job was in a bad way to say the least. The young hooligans mocked him, spit on him, and physically attacked him; this was bad enough. But worse still was the fact that God remained silent and did not answer him. Poor Job! He felt he was alone!

5. JOB ASSERTS AND DEMONSTRATES HIS INTEGRITY (31:1-40)

In chapter 31, Job sets forth the grandest statement of his innocence; in fact, the grandest to be found anywhere in all of Scripture. In chapter 29 he had listed his recollections of how things were in the past. Then in chapter 30 he depicted how painful all his present troubles and miseries were. But now in chapter 31 Job begins with an oath as he tries to show how the accusations of his so-called comforters are totally untrue and not at all accurate. In order to uphold his integrity of life and ethics, Job points to the covenant he had made in the past (31:1), and to his use of the following literary form: 'If I [or 'my steps/ heart' am/are guilty]' (31:5, 7, 9, 13, 16, 19, 20 (bis), 21,24, 25, 26, 38, 39), which was often followed by the imprecation 'let [such and such happen to me]' (31:6, 8, 10, 22, 40). These assertions were not made in an arrogant or self-vaunting manner or style. He was only trying to show how false the charges against him really were.

The crimes listed in chapter 31 were not of the type that one would think were the most noxious set of major wrongs, but they focused on small deviations from the ethical norms and piety that God still required. This list of wrongs went to the deepest level of one's conscience. If Job could show he was innocent at those levels, then surely, he could not be charged with larger crimes that stemmed from those more penetrating motives in the inner person of Job. Thus, Job outlined his case for his extrication on three levels: on the level of his sensual desires or presumed dishonesty towards others (31:1-12), on the level of his possible abuse of power against his slaves, the poor, or the infirmed (31:13-23), and on the level of supposed dishonesty towards God or man (31:24-40).

A. Job's denial of having indulged in lust or dishonesty (31:1-12)

Job was committed to a covenant he had made with his eyes: he would 'not ... look lustfully at a girl' (31:1). Job knew that such a look could lead to acts of sin, therefore he decided to put a block on the very source of such a sin – this he did by making a pledge with his eyes (cf. Prov. 6:25; Matt. 5:28). The 'heritage' or judgment that would come on such a person sinning in this way would bring ruin and calamity (2, 3), since God observes all that goes on down on earth (4).

Job also denied he had indulged in falsehood (5-8), for just as his eyes were free of lustful looks, so his feet were likewise free of being involved in practicing deceit. So convinced was Job of his integrity and that he had kept to God's path of righteousness that he was willing to release the results of his work on his farm to others, instead of eating from the crops he had sown (7-8).

Neither did Job fall into the sin of adultery (9-12), for had his heart enticed him to camp out at his neighbor's door, in order to get a chance to sleep with his neighbor's wife, Job declared that then his wife would be a slave to his neighbor's sexual appetite or grind his grain for him (10). But what kind of a man would subject his wife to such a curse (Deut. 28:30)? Such a fire of adultery would in this case burn in a person's bones so that they would be on the point of being destroyed 'Abaddon,' i.e., 'destruction.' It would consume a man's soul, reputation, body, conscience, family, future, and even the yield of his crops would be decimated (11-12). But Job had not indulged in this sin either!

B. Job's humane treatment of his slaves, the poor, or the infirm (31:13-23)

Job did own a large number of slaves (1:3), but if they had grievances against him, he insisted on hearing their complaints (13), which he was always open to solving. There were two reasons why he acted this way: (1) Job had to answer to God for all his actions, including the way he treated his slaves, and (2) was it not true that both he and his slaves were made by the same God in the womb of a woman (15)? The difference in social strata was not a legitimate basis for showing partiality to some and not to others.

Added to so many other charges, was the charge Eliphaz had made in 22:7-9 that Job had failed to help those in need, such as the poor, widows, orphans or the needy. But Job's help to these very same outcasts of society was the reason God had so blessed Job in the past (29:12-17). In fact, Job had not overlooked the requests of the poor, nor did he let the needs of the widow, the orphan, or the needy go unrequited (16-21). If they needed bread, or the fleece from his sheep to keep warm, they were given it. Job never pulled rank on the 'fatherless' in court (i.e., by 'raising his hand'), for had he done so, he would take an imprecation on his arm that it would fall off his shoulder (22). Job had such a high respect for the Lord, that out of fear for the Lord and His splendor and majesty, he refrained from doing such things to the poor and needy (23).

C. Job denied all other forms of dishonesty to God or man (31:24-40)

This man's security did not rest in his wealth or fortune (24-25). And he certainly did not fall into the idolatry of bowing down to the sun, the moon, and stars (26-28), for then he 'would have been unfaithful to God on high' (28b). Neither was Job a man to get gleeful over the trouble that came to his enemies (29-30), nor could one drop off at Job's door the charge that he was stingy and miserly (31-32). Job did not attempt to hide his sin, or act hypocritical before the crowds of men or women (33-34).

But Job did have one over-riding request: he longed for someone to hear him out (35-37). It was almost as if he signed his name to his oath of innocence in 35b. He wanted any and all accusations against him to be put into writing. Job was so sure that he would be cleared of any incriminations against him that he welcomed his day in court.

The chapter ends with verses 38-40 appearing to be misplaced or somewhat anti-climactic. However, Job feels that if he deserves anything he was suffering, then even his land would be a witness against him and the furrows left from his plowing the earth would figuratively well up with tears against him (38). He was sure he had not eaten of the fruit of his land without paying his laborers. Had he done so, Job wished that briars would come up instead of wheat – but he was not guilty of such injustices.

With such confident words, Job rests his case. His long speeches end with the conclusion: 'The words of Job are ended' (40c). And so they had!

Conclusions

1. At the center of this book is its argument in Job 28, and its search for the wisdom and understanding which can only come from God. Little has changed for many of us today. We too need wisdom!

2. That wisdom and understanding can only be found in the 'fear of the Lord' and in our staying away from evil. Only God knows the way to finding wisdom and understanding.

3. Only God Himself can teach us about His power. Otherwise, all talk is meaningless and a waste of time.

4. Life for Job could be clearly contrasted between 'then' of his former days and the times introduced by 'But now.'

5. Job had made a covenant with his eyes not to look lustfully on a girl. One need not fear the real ruin and disaster that awaits us, unless we do not avoid this evil at its source in our eye gates!

6. Job could say with confidence that he had not failed God even at the level of his motives and heart attitude. No wonder God had selected him as His parade example before Satan!

QUESTIONS FOR REFLECTION
AND DISCUSSION

1. What similarities can you detect between mining in the earth for metals or jewels and the search for wisdom and understanding? Why are so many devoid of wisdom after they have paid expensive tuition rates in schools of higher learning to obtain this wisdom and understanding?

2. What contrasts can you point to in your own life between how you lived before a tragedy or disaster overtook you and how you have lived after that time?

3. What strikes you most in the list of sins that Job lists in Job 31 and the sins of our own day? In what ways are today's list of sins ones that emanate from the heart and interior of a person before they begin to show up externally?

4. Is Job's desire to have God answer him legitimate? Why was God holding back, if that is so?

5. What guilt, or sin, would you charge Job with if his 'Ash-Heap-Trio' was so incorrect?

Chapter 9:
Job 32–34

Young Elihu gives two of his answers to Job

'My words come from an upright heart; my lips sincerely speak what I know' (Job 33:3).

By now Job has learned that God is much greater than Job's words or his theology. If Job or his three friends thought they knew how God would respond to every situation in life, they had a surprise coming to them, even as we will have one coming to us for similar conclusions. God does not fit into our nice little categories or boxes, for He often exceeds the forms and the directions we thought He would take.

1. ELIHU INTRODUCES HIMSELF TO JOB WHILE RESPONDING TO THE ASH-HEAP-TRIO (32:1-22)

True, Job has posed what he thought were some tough questions for God, which in itself is not a problem, for the fact of the matter is that many of Job's questions are similar to our own questions today. Our Lord does not mind answering tough questions, for He answered Moses' tough questions until Moses just quit asking goof questions! However, Job's problem was deeper, for he never lets go of his faith in the fact that God rules this universe, which is wise on his part. However, when Job starts to ask questions that cross the line, it is always about God's apparent delay in answering his request to present his case in front of the Lord. In this way, we are much like Job, for we too impatiently ask the 'Why?' question, often demanding an immediate response whenever pain or suffering hits us. Moreover, what Job lacked in examining his sufferings is precisely what we lack as well: we want to know: 'Why should I have to suffer in this way and why is it taking so long to give me an explanation as to why I have got to wait for an answer?' We, like Job, get so involved in defending ourselves that we forget who God is, and we start demanding answers to our suffering right away without any delay. Too often, like Job we insist on justifying ourselves. But on that point Job, like us, must stop making the case for himself. Our Defender, the Lord Jesus, can and will make the case for us, but He will do so in His own time and in His own way and for His purposes. Thus, as the text of Job 31:40 ends, so do the words of Job and the words of his three visitors (32:1). With that conclusion, a whole new turn of events is introduced in this book, first with the words of a young man named Elihu, the son of Barakel, which means 'God [*Elohim*] blesses.' This conversation is followed with some seventy or more questions for Job from Yahweh and it all concludes with a closing epilogue to the book of Job. Let us follow these final stages carefully.

A. Elihu, the fourth speaker is introduced (32:1-6a)

Here in Job 32:1-6a, the long-running poetic style seen in Job 3:1-42:6 is momentarily broken by a brief prose section to introduce a fourth speaker in 32:1-6a. Elihu, whose name means 'My God is he,' is called a 'Buzite,' so he must have been related to Abraham, since Buz was a brother of Uz, and a son of Nahor, who was Abraham's brother (Gen. 22:20-21). The lands of Buz and Uz were named for these two brothers who lived in the days of Abraham. Elihu also came from the 'family of Ram,' which could mean he was also an ancestor of David, who came later (Ruth 4:19-22).

Elihu begins his speeches by exploding with anger over the fact that Job constantly, but improperly, in his view, insisted on 'justifying himself rather than God' (32:2). Elihu is also angry with Job's three 'comforters' 'because they found no way to refute Job, and yet had condemned him' (3). However, Elihu manages to hold his peace through all of the preceding long discussion between Job and his three friends, because the three men 'were older than he' (4). But when the three men 'had nothing more to say' (5), his anger was stirred up all the more, so he decides it is time for him to enter into the discussion.

So Elihu makes his entry into the conversation with the words: 'I am young in years and you are old' (6). How long this debate had been going on before Elihu enters it is any one's guess, but surely it had extended over a period of days, or possibly even over some months by now. We also do not know how many other listeners were silent observers to this whole dialogue.

Some, however, have unfairly interpreted Elihu's anger as evidence that he was rather impetuous, impulsive, quick-tempered and possessed of a rather pompous style found mainly in young bucks, but the text does not support this assessment of Elihu. As a matter of fact, he waited patiently and quietly for a lull in the debate before he dared to enter into it. Therefore, rather than attributing to Elihu the arrogance and impetuosity of youth, as some have mistakenly done, or worse still, of seeing his contributions as smart-alec remarks that imitated and parroted back what his seniors had already said, some have more accurately regarded Elihu's argument as constituting the very core and the heart of the argument of this book. Ray Steadman,[1] in particular, listed four arguments for viewing Elihu as the one who really had come to grips with what the book of Job was all about. Steadman's four arguments were these:

1. God did not rebuke Elihu, as he did rebuke Job's other three friends in the conclusion to the book for the foolish things they had said. In Job 42:7 the Lord uttered these words to Eliphaz: 'I am angry with you and your two friends, because you have not spoken of me what is right, as my servant Job has.' But there was, however, no word of reprimand for Elihu at all. Why?

2. Elihu's message is given a prominent place in the drama of this book, for he is given six whole chapters (Job 32-37), making it one of the longest discourses in the whole book. Since God did not single out Elihu for condemnation, this therefore seemed to be more than a tacit endorsement of his views.

---

1. Ray Stedman, *Let God Be God: Life-Changing Truth from the Book of Job*, Grand Rapids, MI.: Discovery House Publishers, 2007 (eBook 2014) at the 66% - 67% level [or: "Elihu: A Misunderstood Young Man, Job 32:).

3. Unlike Job's other three friends, who were often caustic, sarcastic, and ones who showed little or no empathy for Job's pain and suffering, Elihu appears to be more sensitive to Job's situation.

4. Whereas Job's three friends tended to speak from their position of age or experience, Elihu claimed to speak from the vantage point of a revelation that came from God.

Elihu's first speech does not actually begin until 33:1, for it is preceded in 32:6-22 by his rather lengthy defense of his intrusion into the debate. This wordy introduction must be examined then before we undertake an examination of his speeches.

B. Elihu's respect for Job's three counselors (32:6-10)

Given his youthful age, Elihu sees himself as shy and somewhat apprehensive about butting in on the conversation with his own opinion (6). He feels that age and advanced years should be given priority in the order of speaking (7). However, Elihu also realizes that it is the Spirit of God who gives a person understanding (8), for one cannot say that 'only the old ... are wise,' and 'only the aged [are those] who understand what is right' (9). Consequently, given these truths, Elihu dares to declare: 'Listen to me; I too will tell you what I know' (10).

C. Elihu's evaluation of Job's three counselors (32:11-14)

He has listened very closely to the 'reasoning' each of the three men have offered Job as these men 'search[ed] for words,' 'But not one of [them had] proved Job wrong;

none of [them had] answered his arguments,' Elihu chides (11-12). Therefore, the three men of the 'Ash-Heap Trio' should not claim that they have 'found wisdom,' nor should they have gone on to argue that God will refute Job, who is a mortal like themselves (13). This is why Elihu will not take the approach and the line of argumentation that the three men had taken, for he will not use their arguments at all to respond to Job (14). Elihu is candid in his assessment of what the three had been able to accomplish; however, his tone to them and to Job is still courteous even as he continues to explain why he feels he has to speak.

D. Elihu explains why he felt he must speak to Job (32:15-22)
Elihu assumes he has silenced the three men, for they have nothing more to say. He then, though being much younger than them, gives his opinion on this discussion (15-17), for he is 'full of words' (18a) – few readers of this text would disagree with him on that point! He announces, instead, that who was impelling him to speak, is none other than the Spirit of God (18). For a second reason he feels so strongly about what he is about to say is that he is like a bottled-up jug of wine that is about to explode even though it has been poured into new wineskins (19). A third reason he is urged to contribute to this dialogue is this: if he didn't speak up he would find no relief, for he just had 'to open his lips and reply' (20). The final reason he gives is that he has refused to show any partiality to anyone in this debate, for he simply refuses either to flatter Job or his three friends (21-22). Accordingly, Elihu wants all to know that he has no intention of flattering anyone or attempting to gain anyone's favor; he will only speak

what the Holy Spirit revealed to him from the Lord his Maker. Could this, then, be the answer from God that Job has been seeking?

2. THE FIRST OF ELIHU'S FOUR SPEECHES (33:1-33)
The new young participant in the discussion begins with an invitation to Job to 'listen' and to 'pay attention to everything' that he (Elihu) is going to say (33:1).

A. Elihu urges Job to pay close attention to all he is going to say (33:1-7)
Instead of speaking in order to flatter or merely to condemn Job, Elihu requests that Job heed the very words God has given to him. So different is the tone Elihu uses from that of Job's three counselors that the contrast can be seen immediately. Elihu claims his words come from 'an upright heart' and are spoken 'sincerely' (3). Neither does this young man exalt himself and place himself on a higher pedestal than Job, for both he and Job are God's creations, for had not the same God given to both of them life (4).

Therefore, since all mortals are equal before God, and since all have been made out of clay, Job didn't have to fear that Elihu was going to be harsh with him, nor would he try to bully him into his selective way of thinking, for 'my hand will [not] be heavy on you' (7). Elihu just was not going to browbeat Job or accuse him as the other three men had done.

B. Elihu examines what Job had said about God (33:8-13)
First of all, Elihu had heard Job make this assertion:

181

'I am pure and without sin; I am clean and free of guilt.
Yet God has found fault with me; he considers me his
enemy' (9-10).

There was no question about the fact that Job was indeed
a godly man, yet due to his suffering he had fallen into a
narrow view of God, which in some ways paralleled the
view his friends had adopted. Instead of remembering
that God's ways are not our ways, Job began instead to
view God from his own human standpoint and limited
perspective. Job should not have projected his own self-
image onto God. God is infinitely greater than any of
Job's, or our, understandings. In so doing, Job had begun
to talk back to God as the Apostle Paul warned we must
not do under any circumstances (Rom. 9:20).

Elihu quietly offers this rebuke: 'But I tell you [Job], in
this you are not right, for God is greater than man' (12).
Job had forgotten that God's plans and purposes are much
more extensive and deeper than Job's plans for himself
or our plans for ourselves. Job was incorrect in laying the
charge of capriciousness at the feet of our Lord. Of course,
we too are often just as guilty of demanding quick and
immediate responses from our Lord when we pray. It might
have been five minutes, five hours, or five days ago when
we prayed for an answer, but we often begin to despair of
hearing God's answer to our prayers, because that answer
does not come at the time we demand, or exactly with the
response we had hoped for. God does not owe any of us
an immediate answer. Elihu, on the other hand, gives a
different perspective on God's answers, for he informs Job,
and us, by divine revelation that 'God does speak – now in

one way, now in another – though man may not perceive it' (14). So, God was answering Job's inquiries all during those days of suffering! Job just was not alert to what God was doing!

C. Elihu explains two of the ways God speaks to us (33:14-28)
Our young speaker informs Job, as he simultaneously informs us, that there are two ways God speaks to us: he often speaks to us through dreams[2] (15-18), or he may speak through our pain and suffering (19-28). Earlier in this debate, Eliphaz, the senior spokesman of the three, had used the vehicle of a spooky dream (without saying whether the dream was from God or himself) to point out to men and women their sins and impurities (4:12-21), but Elihu refers to dreams as the way in which God teaches mortals how to live and thereby keep them from sinning against heaven! It is in our dreams, he teaches, that God opens our ears (16a), and He warns us of possible wrongdoing (16b). Whereas we mortals all too often are bent on doing something that is antithetical to the call of God, He lovingly warns us through our dreams, thus sparing us from greater distress and pain. This is not an exhortation to start analyzing all of our dreams, as if they all were a message from God, but it is to say that some of our dreams may represent God speaking to us, while other dreams, of course, may come from eating too much food too late in the evening!

---

2. See 'Dreams.' Edwin M. Yamauchi, *Dictionary of Daily Life in Biblical and Post-Biblical Antiquity,* (Hendrickson Publishers, Massachusetts, 2016).

Elihu also teaches that God answered Job and He answers us through our pain (19-28). Elihu makes a surprising statement here, for he asserts that God has been answering Job all along, even though Job thought God had been silent. This was not to concede the point that Job's pain and suffering was because Job had some hidden sin in his life, as his three friends persisted in affirming. That was not true at all; but Job was just plain wrong in thinking that God had been silent all during his affliction. After all, pain is one of God's ways of getting our attention.

Steadman was right to call to our attention C.S. Lewis' way of making this point in *The Problem of Pain*. There Lewis commented:

> We can rest contentedly in our sins and in our stupidities, ... [for] anyone who has watched gluttons shoveling down the most exquisite foods as if they did not know what they were eating, will admit that we can ignore even pleasure. But pain insists upon being attended to. God whispers to us in our pleasures, speaks in our consciences, but shouts in our pains. It is his megaphone to rouse a deaf world.[3]

It is true, of course, that the teaching we get from dreams is mostly negative, while that which comes from angels, who arrive in times of pain, is more often positive (23). Here Elihu refers to a 'Mediator,' 'one of the thousand' (23), who in this case just may have been a Christophony. Already we have seen this Messianic figure under the various names such as an 'Adjudicator' (9:33), a 'Witness' (16:19), and a 'Kinsmen-Redeemer' (19:25-27). Here Messiah appears as

---

3. C.S. Lewis, *The Problem of Pain*, (HarperCollins e-book, 2009), pp. 91-92.

a 'Mediator' who comes 'to tell a man what is right for him' (23c). This Mediator 'spare[s] him from going down to the pit' ('pit,' a word used for the 'grave' four times in this chapter), because he has 'found a ransom for him' (24b-c). The person in pain and suffering finds, as a result of the Mediator's work, that 'his flesh is renewed like a child's; it is restored as in the days of his youth' (25). The restoration promised by Elihu, as a result of this man's prayer, is the favor and joy of seeing God face to face and being restored to his righteous state (26). This sounds like nothing less than the beautiful benefits that come as a result of the Gospel itself. Even the person who comes and admits that he or she has sinned and gone the wrong way away from God, can obtain this gift of grace. Yet some surprisingly do not get what they deserve, for God redeems their soul from going down to the pit (i.e., 'the grave.') (27-28). What an unexpected gift!

D. Elihu makes his appeal to Job (33:29-33)
Elihu chides Job to speak up, for if he has anything to say, please do so now at this time (32). Instead of Elihu's arguing as Job's three friends had that suffering was retributive, Elihu now argues that Job's suffering is protective, for it keeps mortals from death. God does this repeatedly ('twice, even three times'), that is, He holds back mortals from going down to the pit so they could experience the 'light of life ... shin[ing] on [them]' (29-30). Suffering then is not always a punishment for the sins a person has committed, but suffering and pain are used as one of God's ways of gaining our attention and steering us clear of sin. Job's 'Ash-Heap-Trio' wanted Job

to repent of his sin so that God could restore him back to His divine favor, but Elihu's solution was different: it was instead that he was to listen to the Angel from God, who would remind him how it is that he was to live and thereby be restored to the Lord. Of course, depending on the situation, Job's friends and Elihu were both correct, for at times God uses suffering as a means of judging us for our sins, but at other times He uses suffering as a means of preventing us from going all the way to experiencing death itself. In light of this goodness from God, we mortals need to humble ourselves under His mighty, but gracious hand!

3. THE SECOND OF ELIHU'S FOUR SPEECHES (34:1-37)

A. Elihu examines Job's second complaint with his friends (34:1-9)

In his second speech Elihu takes up Job's second problem with God; i.e., that God is unjust. As he does so, he addresses Job's three conversation partners, as can be seen from his references to 'you wise men' (2), 'you men of understanding,' and the plural pronoun 'you.' Later Elihu will speak directly to Job in 34:16-37 as the singular pronoun 'you' demonstrates.

Elihu recalls Job's claim of innocence as he requests his three elderly speakers to listen to him and to decide whether he or Job is correct (2-4):

> Job says. 'I am innocent, but God denied me justice. Although I am right, I am considered a liar; although I am guiltless, [God's] arrow inflicts an incurable wound' (34:5-6).

It is true that Job had made assertions similar to these, even if Elihu quotes him indirectly. Job had claimed: 'I am righteous' (13:18; 27:6; 34:5a); he had inferred: 'I am without transgression' (13:23; 14:17; 23:11; 34:6b); and he had said outrightly: 'God has taken away my [legal] right' (27:2; 34:5b; cf. 34:6a). Wow! Were Job's three 'counselors' right after all? Was Elihu now siding with them and conceding their case (34:7); such as in an allusion perhaps to Eliphaz's speech in 15:16?

Elihu summarizes Job's whole point as one that rests in his second charge: 'It profits a man nothing when he tries to please God' (34:9). Is Job correct in this? Will Elihu let that charge stand?

B. Elihu refutes Job's second charge (34:10-37)

Elihu thinks it is 'unthinkable that God would actually do wrong, [or] that the Almighty would pervert justice' (10). In fact, God is just and fair in giving to mortals what they deserve (11); He is answerable to no one, for no one has appointed Him as Lord over the earth (13); He is the One who gave life to mortals and He it is who has the power to withdraw life as well (14-15); He is the One who declares kings to be worthless and allows nobles to be wicked without showing partiality (16-20); He is the One who in His omniscience sees all the ways of mortals without the benefit of a court case to investigate their realities or without bringing up all these details out in the open (21-25a); and He is the One who overthrows the wicked in the night, and those who were in public places, He also overthrew during the day, i.e., all those who showed no regard for His ways (25b-30).

Elihu, however, had some tough words for Job, for he asserts:

> What man is like Job, who drinks scorn like water? He keeps company with evildoers; he associates with wicked men. For he says, 'It profits a man nothing when he tries to please God' (34:7-9).

Elihu's harsh rebuke does not seem to match Job's initial response when he was first hit by affliction. Did he not say the following on that occasion?

> Naked I came from my mother's womb, and naked I will depart. The LORD gave and the LORD has taken away; may the name of the LORD be praised (1:21).

But now Elihu summarizes Job's latest position as 'It profits a man nothing when he tries to please God' (34:9). Job seems to be saying now that it does no good to walk in the ways of the Lord; one may as well just indulge oneself in evil and sin, because God does not notice or reward those who please Him. Elihu was afraid of the place to which Job's doubts were beginning to lead him. Job had not cursed God, as Satan had wagered, sure enough, but he was getting perilously close to falling into Satan's trap and doing just that.

But Job has to be reminded of the fact that God will judge the wicked and bless the righteous. The scales of divine justice may not balance out immediately and as quickly as Job would like, but God will never fail to demonstrate His justice in His own time and in His own way. Elihu teaches that God will act justly in accordance with His nature. God's character does not fluctuate, for

He is unchangeable in the character of His being and thus in His actions. However, since God is all-wise and infinite in His being, He is accountable to no mortal or to any other alleged competitor! Furthermore, God knows each one of us completely, and He does not have to give an account to anyone.

Given such high views of God, Elihu wants to know how any mere mortal might have the nerve to demand from God an accounting for his actions and decisions. He puts it this way:

> But if [God] remains silent, who can condemn him? If he hides his face, who can see? Yet he is over man and nation alike, to keep a godless man from ruling, from laying snares for the people. Suppose a man says to God, 'I am guilty, but will offend no more. Teach me what I cannot see; if I have done wrong, I will not do so again.' Should God then reward you on your terms, when you refuse to repent? You must decide, not I; so, tell me what you know. (34:29-33).

God will not stand for questioning of His decisions by any of us, not even by Job, for He is a Sovereign God who stands supreme over all individuals and nations. Nor can He be put off by the offer of substitutes for righteousness. If some think they can come to God on their own terms with their own substitutions for the way of salvation, their alternatives are just not acceptable to God nor will it be a real salvation. God is not looking to merely reform us, but He wants to renew us thoroughly; He seeks our genuine and sincere total repentance, not our promises of some sort of change or reform in the future. Neither does our

Lord look for us merely to say we will never do such and such a thing again; He wants a wholehearted and absolute surrender that turns our lives over to Him.

Elihu closes his second speech in verses 34-37 by teaching Job that he has spoken out of ignorance of who God really is. It is for this reason that Job needs to be tested some more! This claim for more testing startles us, for we think Job has been through too much already! It seems as if Elihu is now being cruel to the limits. This is an outrageous position on Elihu's part, or so we think.

But Elihu is not primarily interested in increasing Job's problems; he only wants him to be brought to the truth. His point is this: If one's suffering results in a person knowing God better, then let Job be tested until he no longer demands that his own righteousness be recognized, but instead he depends solely and totally on God's righteousness! But up to this point, Job thinks that he can achieve his own righteousness by his own efforts. Job has failed to recognize the fact that evil still lurks even in what he viewed as his own righteousness. Was it not the prophet Isaiah who on another occasion taught that 'all our righteous acts are like filthy rags, … and like the wind our sins sweep us away' (Isa. 64:6). The truth is that none of our efforts are adequate to grant us favor in God's eyes. We, like Job, are willing to grant that we are sinners, but we also think, that on the whole, we are not that bad, and we are usually pretty good people, especially if examined alongside of others. If we generally obey God's Word, isn't it only fair to think that God will reward us for our good achievements?

It is difficult for believers to get their minds around the truth that in God's sight all our righteousness amounts to nothing more than filthy rags. We would prefer to regard that as an exaggerated hyperbole, or as some type of inexplicable metaphor, but it is instead the plain, sober, truth from God.

As we look back on the story of Job as it began in chapter 1, it is important to notice that the idea of testing Job was not Satan's, but it was God's proposition to Satan. God, it appears, was positioning Satan so that He, the Lord Jesus, could achieve His own goals with Job through Satan's actions. Satan thought he would win this argument easily, hands down, that Job served God because he was his blue-eyed boy whom He blessed so regularly, but God knew His man Job would not curse Him or disown Him. However, God loved Job so much that He wanted to bring him to a deeper knowledge of himself. Hence, the pain, suffering and affliction continued for Job!

Conclusions

1. Job continued to be tested by God for two reasons: (1) He wanted to prevent him from going down to the grave with his sins, and (2) because Job was still trusting in his own acts of righteousness and not in the acts of God's righteousness.

2. Elihu may have been the youngest speaker, but he did not follow the same tack as his elders had. He depended on God's revelation and His Holy Spirit to guide his thinking and speaking.

3. God uses both some of our dreams to warn us of trouble up ahead and our pain and suffering to prevent us from falling into the trap of the evil one.

4. Job acknowledges the help of the Angel of the Lord, a 'Mediator,' who will be gracious to him by sparing him from going down to the pit, because he has found a ransom for him.

QUESTIONS FOR REFLECTION
AND DISCUSSION

1. Do you agree that Elihu brings the solution to the problem of Job's suffering contrary to the views of his three elders who preceded him?

2. Did God speak uniquely to Job through 'an angel on his side,' but the question is this: does He use angels to speak to mortals in our day as well? How is this different from our going to a spiritist or palm-reader in our day?

3. What was the difference between Eliphaz's use of an angel appearing in his dream and the way an angel appeared to Elihu?

4. Why did Elihu want God to continue the pain and suffering Job was experiencing, especially when he had already been through so much?

5. What was the difference between the source of Elihu's speeches and the source of the three 'Ash-Heap-Trio's' words?

Chapter 10:
Job 35–37

Young Elihu refutes two more accusations of Job

'Who is a teacher like [God]? ... How great
is God — beyond our understanding!'
(Job 36:22b, 26a)

In Elihu's third speech, he challenges Job once again as he takes up another one of Job's complaints. Elihu asks Job straightforwardly:'

> Do you think this is just? You say, 'I will be cleared by God.' Yet you ask him, 'What profit is it to me, and what do I gain by not sinning?' (35:2-3).

Something is wrong here and Elihu wants to get to the bottom of it.

1. ELIHU REFUTES JOB'S THIRD CHARGE AGAINST GOD (35:1-16)

A. Elihu rises to defend God once more (35:1-8)

We are embarrassed for Job, for he has been claiming that he is still innocent; this is because as he sees it, God is letting him suffer. Of course Job had made such a claim earlier, as he had used similar ideas in 9:30-31. But Job could not pull the wool over Elihu's eyes. Job seems to be thinking that by his living a good and wholesome life for

God, he is doing an enormous favor for God. But God is not all that impressed, for since He is as high above the clouds as the clouds are high above the earth, so Job has nothing to offer God by his good works. God is unaffected one way or the other – that is either in His person or His character – by Job's sins or by his righteousness (35:5-7). Therefore, Job should not think that just because he is suffering that God was acting out of spite against him.

B. Elihu explains why God appears to be indifferent to us (35:9-12)

Mortals cry out to God under the load of their pain, but God surely knows that they cry only for relief and not for the help they need. Most of all, we mortals want the pain and hurt to stop. However, all too often, the moment that the pain is gone, too many of us fall back into our selfish ways and acts of sin – often into the very things that caused our pain and grief in the first place! It is no wonder then, that God's answer often is one of silence (12). Instead of our being concerned for God's righteousness and glory, we are more concerned to get over the penalty for our sins and the selfishness that produced the pile of pain. We want the hurting to stop; but not necessarily the sin or the things we did that caused this agony. Here may be one of the key reasons why our prayers go unanswered: our sins produced the pain that we now cry out to God to for relief. But it is not our concern for God's reputation or glory that motivates our cry for God's intervention: it is rather our selfish desire to have relief from the pain!

Those who cry out for relief often forget that God their Maker (10a) is the One who 'gives songs in the night' (10b).

God is also the One who 'teaches' us and 'makes us wiser than the birds of the air' (11b).

C. God often does not answer our prayers because we do not pray in humility (35:13-16)

All too often our prayers are only prayers for deliverance and not prayers to God borne out of true humility. Oppressors do not seek instructions from God as to how to deal with suffering, but act instead like animals. The motivation behind all too many prayers is one of arrogance and pride (12). Those prayers are not filled with evidence of sincerity and purposefulness; instead, their prayers are just empty pleas filled with hollow and meaningless words with no evidence of knowledge behind those words (15-16). Job had thought that his problem was that God was hidden from him. But Elihu contended on the other hand, that God was not indifferent to Job or to all who were hurting; it was rather the case that Job was speaking emptily and with meaningless words. Elihu was amazed that Job wanted to have a trial before God wherein he would be his own defense attorney. Elihu retorts to such a demand with the question: 'How can you talk like that to God? Who do you think you are, Job? Do you think God is waiting for you to prove Him wrong?' Even though Elihu is gentle with Job, he tells him he is just blabbing a bunch of words that have no solid information behind them to back them up. Why do you want to prove that God is wrong and that you are right, Job? How in the world is God going to be able to respond to such a request from you? Job, you must rethink what you are demanding of God! It is just plain exasperating!

2. ELIHU MAKES HIS MOST IMPRESSIVE SPEECH AGAINST JOB IN HIS RESPONSE TO JOB'S FOURTH CHARGE (36:1–37:24)

A. The justice of God that deals with mortals, both the wicked and afflicted, must be examined first (36:1-15)

Elihu is really at his best in this his fourth and final speech (36:1–37:24). He has indeed already touched on several of the topics he would raise, such as suffering, God's justice, and God's sovereignty in his earlier three talks; but here his speech rises to a new height as his words come close to approximating the grandeur and magnificence of the awesome character of God in all its fullness.

Once more Elihu makes the claim that he will speak from the source of divine authority that informed him (36:2-4). Elihu must think that Job needs to be reminded of the fact that he must begin understanding his pain and suffering by depending on the knowledge of God. Isn't it true, Job, Elihu asks, that God's knowledge is infallible? Consequently everything that deviates from that knowledge must be regarded as false and unreliable! Isn't it also true, Job, that when we begin our thinking and questioning of God from our own ideas and opinions that that is how we start to go astray from the teaching of our Lord? We must agree with what God says; not with what we might say! Here is how Elihu put it:

> Bear with me a little longer and I will show you that there is more to be said on God's behalf. I get my knowledge from afar; I will ascribe justice to my Maker. Be assured that my words are not false: One perfect in knowledge is with you. (36:2-4).

Some insist on charging Elihu with being arrogant and somewhat pompous when he claims: 'my words are not false; One perfect in knowledge is with you' (4). But that assessment of Elihu depends on attributing Elihu's words to himself and is therefore a misinterpretation of the text as I see it. Instead, however, Elihu is speaking only of God as the 'One perfect in knowledge' and not of himself at all, as a glance forward in 37:16 informs us. He wants Job to know that his speech is given on the authority and inspiration of the Lord God Himself! God is not directed by mere mortals, nor is He so flexible and so partial in His standard of justice that it cannot be understood or maintained.

Elihu continues in 36:5 to declare that God is mighty and resolute in His purpose. This verse 5 begins with the attention-grabbing 'Behold' in the Hebrew text, for it is one of the four times in this chapter where Elihu introduces his affirmation on the power of God with the word 'Behold' (Hebrew, *hen*, 36:5, 22, 26, 30). Elihu's point is that God's might comes matched with His mercy as well, for He 'does not despise men' (36:5). God 'does not keep the wicked alive, but he gives to the afflicted their rights' (6). Job had declared just the opposite in 21:27-33, but on that point Job was wrong. Moreover, God 'does not take his eyes off the righteous, [but] he enthrones them with kings and exalts them forever' (7). Yet it must also be said, that if the righteous suffer affliction, God can and will use that affliction to point out their sins, such as pride, and to teach them and command them 'to repent of their evil' (8-10).

However, if men and women 'obey and serve him' (11a), they will enjoy their days and years in 'contentment' and 'prosperity' (11b-c). On the other hand, if men and women 'do not listen' (12a), they will 'perish by the sword' (12b, which is Elihu's expression for death, 33:18) 'and [they will] die without knowledge' (12c). Once again Elihu contrasts the attitudes of the godless with those of the righteous. The wicked get angry with God over their problems and 'harbor resentment' in their hearts (13a), yet they refuse to turn to God in repentance and therefore meet with untimely deaths (14a). Meanwhile the righteous are delivered from their pain and suffering and learn from their afflictions (15a-b).

B. Elihu begins to apply these truths to Job (36:16-25)

It is at this point that Elihu begins to apply these points in 12-15 to Job and his pain and distress (16-25). He first of all makes an extremely important point with Job:

> But those who suffer he (i.e., God) delivers in their suffering; he speaks to them [or literally: (God) opens their ears] in their [time of] affliction' (36:15).

Elihu's emphasis is on the fact that God does more than speak to us when we are afflicted; instead, He uses our trials and afflictions to open our ears so we can hear what He wants to say to us! It is true, as we quoted C. S. Lewis on this point earlier in our study, 'God whispers to us in our pleasures, speaks in our consciences, but shouts in our pain. It is his megaphone to rouse a deaf world.'[1]

---

1. Lewis, p. 92.

Even more dramatically, Elihu continues his teaching of Job by showing him that God is trying to woo and entice him to Himself by calling him out of his confining experience of pain into a spacious place of enormous blessing (16). But for Job to go there, he has to give up his complaint against God that He is unjust (16-17). Elihu points out to Job that he had previously said with some bitterness and resentment that the anguish of his suffering was causing him to begin to turn aside from God (18). Elihu warns that Job's attempt to get rid of his problem of suffering by using some kind of human effort to get him out of this jam, or even to die, would not be the right answer to Job's dilemma (19-20). Don't turn to the sin of complaining, which thus far had been Job's favorite way of dealing with his suffering.

Elihu introduces, for the second time, his attention-calling word, 'Behold' (Hebrew text) in verse 22. Elihu calls Job's attention to God, 'who is to be exalted beyond any and all competitors, and who acted majestically in his power' (22), and therefore answerable to no one. Our Lord just could not be surpassed as a 'Teacher' (Hebrew, *moreh*, 22b; cf. Joel 2:23). Moreover, our God does not need to give an answer to anyone, thus He is not challengeable by any mortal. He consistently does all that is good and right (22-23). It is for this reason that Job should magnify God for all He has done. Yes, and this is also the reason why all mortals should sing praises to Him, for His majestic works are available for mortals to gaze upon from afar (24-25). Elihu seems to be implying another principle for Job to digest: when mortals adore God as rightfully the majestic, powerful, sovereign Teacher, they have fewer occasions for indulging in self-pity and for complaining about how God has not answered them.

For the third time in this chapter, Elihu begins with the introductory word 'Behold,' that calls everyone's attention to what is coming next in God's revelation (26). Elihu moves towards concluding his final speech (now numbering four) with a hymn that mightily exalts the glory and power of God (36:22–37:24). This hymn includes at the very inception of its adoration a note of praise to the greatness of God which goes way beyond our understanding (36:26) and continues through chapter 37, ending with a similar statement in 37:22b-23) of praise for God's 'awesome majesty.'

The greatness of God exceeds every ounce of our ability to comprehend his magnificence (36:26a); for it goes way beyond even our ability to understand even such simple processes as the process of evaporation (27-28). No less powerful and magnificent are the clouds and the role of thunder (29), or even the workings God possesses in His use of lightning and the way His thunderbolts bounce off the depths of the sea (30). God also uses His governance of the nations to feed all creatures here below (31). He divinely fills His hands with lightning and commands it to strike its mark (32), for often the roar of thunder announces that a storm is about to break over the land; it is a sign of the divine presence, a fact that even cattle show an awareness of as the storm approaches (33).

The depiction of a possible actual electrical storm, with its awesome and powerful presence, is eloquently continued as we move into chapter 37. So impressed is Elihu with the presence and power of this storm that his heart races with fear as it 'leaps from its place' at the sound of the storm's rumbling and the clashing echoed in its thunder claps one after another (37:1). Elihu could have seen the same teaching in such texts as Psalm 29:3, 4, 5, 7, 8, 9, which likewise viewed the clamor of the thunder as nothing less than the majestic 'voice of God,' (3-5). When God unleashes His thunder and lightning, He 'holds nothing back' (4d), for He is in the process of doing 'great things beyond our understanding' (5b). Job too has already spoken of this very same thunder as being nothing less than God's 'mighty thunder' and His voice (26:14).

Elihu also points in verses 6-7 to how a heavy snowfall, or a downpour of rain, coming as well at the command of God, can 'stop every man from his labor.' Mortals are familiar with such impediments, for many have often been driven from their labor in the fields by a heavy rainstorm and others have seen how a heavy snowfall or a blizzard will snarl traffic or sequester folks in their homes for days at a time. Even the animals take cover in their dens during such weather patterns as well (8) when 'the breath of God produces ice' or frost (9-10). Indeed, the very clouds of the sky along with the storms in the natural world are controlled by God (11-12). No human being could control or regulate the weather or such storms; only God is in charge of these elements which He has stored up often in great quantities in His heavenly reservoirs.

Elihu does not break off his teaching at this point without showing its relevance to Job, for he wants once again to apply it to Job specifically in this section of 14-24. Job must come to realize four principles: First of all Job must be awed and deeply impressed by the magnificence of God (14-18); secondly, Job cannot demand to have God personally attend his court case at his human timing and on his earthly command (19-20); thirdly, he cannot directly see God and have his chance to explain his case personally (21-23); and finally, he must fear and revere God (24).

In order to help Job understand the points he is making, Elihu asks a series of questions that will help him to realize his inadequacies before an Almighty God. This will also prepare him for the heavy questioning he will face shortly from the Lord God Himself. To begin with, Elihu asks if Job knows how God controls the clouds (15a)? Does Job also know how God controls the lightning and makes it flash (15b)? Or Job, Elihu continues, do you know how God suspends and hangs, as it were, the clouds in the air, even though they are heavily water-logged (16)? These questions reflect the character and work of One who is 'perfect in knowledge' (16b). Obviously these questions are not haphazard or randomly selected inquiries; instead they each have a purpose behind them. In some of these instances, God might use them to bring judgment on some, or on the other hand, to be the means of bringing blessing to the earth (13). But then again, God might use a storm for His own purposes, for He is free to do whatever He pleases without being forced to give an explanation to mortals for everything He does.

Job has continued to long for an opportunity to 'arrange' and to present his case before God (13:18), but the truth is, as Elihu reminds Job, that mortals are just plain incapable of approaching God directly 'because of our darkness' (37:19b). To show how ludicrous such an approach to God would be, Elihu challenges Job to tell all who listen to him 'what [any of them] should say to [God]' if they dare to approach him (19a). None of them, not even Job would know what to say! Therefore, if Job cannot adequately comprehend such common occurrences in nature such as the flashing of lightning, the clouds filled with rain-water, or the arrival of hot south wind, how on earth does he find the nerve to pretend he could defend himself before such an awesome God? Even if someone merely said he wanted to speak with God, 'would [not that] man be swallowed up' (20b)? To think that a person could make a case in his or her own self-defense would be a quick way to experience self-destruction!

Elihu takes Job back to consider the skies once more. As the wind sweeps the skies clean of its clouds and storms, so our Lord comes 'out of the north in golden splendor' (22a) and 'in awesome majesty' (22b). Just what this 'golden splendor out of the north' is we cannot say for sure. The major point however is clear: 'The Almighty is beyond our reach and [he is] exalted in power' (23a).

Elihu brings his speech to its highest point as he concludes by praising God for His awesome majesty and splendor. That gives him occasion to emphasize two characteristics of God to Job: God's sovereignty, for He is 'exalted in power' (23a), and His justice and righteousness, for 'he does not oppress' (23b). Elihu's assertion about God's justice stands in direct opposition to Job's repeated and unfair accusation that God is not true (7:20; 9:17; 10:2-3; 13:24; 16:9, 12, 17; 19:6-12; 27:2; 30:19-28). On Elihu's point about God's power, however, Job is in agreement (9:4-12 etc).

Elihu makes one final recommendation to Job: Fear this awesome and powerful Lord. If Job is anywhere near being as wise as he should be, he would revere God as the One wise in heart (9:4). Elihu has done his job by now, for he has prepared the way for the Lord God to speak.

Conclusions

1. Job had come close to doing exactly what Satan wanted him to do, but thanks be to God, he stopped short of doing so on several occasions.

2. God is sovereign over all men and nations. And while He is mighty in strength and firm in His purpose, yet He does not despise mortals.

3. God is a Teacher par excellence. That is another reason why we ought to be praising His greatness, for He goes way beyond our understanding.

4. God speaks to mortals through the roar and clap of the thunder and lightning, yet we are usually too slow to hear His voice or to be still in His presence.

5. The wonders of God's person are enormous, for no one even comes close to Him in the perfection of His knowledge.

QUESTIONS FOR REFLECTION
AND DISCUSSION

1. What makes Elihu's speeches so different from those of the three who spoke ahead of him? Does Elihu's case make the central point of the book?

2. In your estimation, did Elihu speak with the advantage of speaking out of his understanding of the divine revelation or was he a sort of pompous guy who loved to show off what little he knew?

3. What was the principled teaching of Elihu's questions and how did they affect Job and the case he was trying to make?

4. What in Elihu's final speech pointed to the greatness and awesome majesty of God?

5. Is the word for 'Teacher' in 36:22 a true Messianic figure? If so, why? If not, why not?

Chapter 11:
Job 38:1–39:30

God challenges Job:
Part 1

'Where were you when I laid the earth's foundations?' (Job 38:4)

Suddenly what Job has been longing to happen takes place as God speaks directly to Job out of the midst of a storm (38:1). Here is the moment that Job has wanted so badly to happen; God is now answering him out of the raging storm. But the encounter between God and Job is not nearly as comfortable and as smooth as Job might have originally pictured it in his mind! The opening word from the mouth of the Lord immediately tells Job that God has not viewed his words up to this point to be words filled with knowledge. In fact, the initial word from the Almighty to Job is a question that goes like this:

> Who is this that darkens my counsel with words without knowledge? (38:2).

Despite the fact that this question is clearly placed in the context of the Lord directly speaking to Job out of a storm that is in progress (38:1), some commentators think that perhaps God is saying something like this:

> Who is this young man [Elihu] who has been speaking to you and who darkens my counsel with such ignorant words?

But this way of redirecting the question to Elihu instead of addressing it to Job, clearly violates the context of Scripture. Moreover, in Job 42:3, it was Job himself who later confesses the following apology when he replied to the Lord:

> You asked, 'Who is this that obscures my counsel without knowledge?' Surely I spoke of things I did not understand, things too wonderful for me to know.

Indeed, the Lord God is addressing none other than Job himself when He begins to question him in Job 38:2, and not Elihu, as some incorrectly advocate. Job is the man on the spot according to God's words and not Elihu!

It is with this initial question that the Lord reprimands Job for obscuring His counsel and plans with words that reflect ignorance and not with the wisdom that comes from the Lord on high. One wonders how frequently the same darkening of God's Word takes place from those who claim to love Him, teach and preach about Him, but who have attributed unsupported meanings to Scripture that do not fit the context or the truth that the Holy Spirit means to communicate in the text of Scripture that they presume to be teaching from, or teaching what these teachers are saying!

Moreover, to add to the drama, God appears in the midst of a storm in progress, as He often does in Scripture (Exod. 19:16-17; 1 Kings 19:11-13; Isa. 6:4; Ezek. 1:4;

and Zech. 9:14). So, God begins Job's long-awaited retort by challenging the validity of Job's insights. Just as the electrical storm may have brought an overcast darkness with it, so all too much of what has been said about God is filled with just plain darkness and ignorance! Thus, God begins by accusing Job of downright ignorance and a lack of knowledge. Whereas Job might have thought that he was in a position to stand up for the ways of God and to vindicate them to those ill-informed about the same, God has heard Job's speeches and He has found them deficient. That complaint could be laid out in the following fashion.

Job charges God with dealing with him in an unfair and unjust way. But such a charge means that Job is speaking without knowledge and without an adequate awareness of the real facts in this case. It is for this reason that the Lord demands that Job 'Brace himself like a man,' or more literally to 'gird up [his] loins like a man,' which means it is time for Job to pick up his long robe and tuck it into his belt as he gets ready for action, which in this case is the action of the mind and of thought. Yes, the time has come for Job to give an account of himself to God. Job had thought all along that he was the plaintiff in this case before God; however, it suddenly turns out that he is the defendant! Job is to be subjected to a bewildering barrage of some seventy penetrating questions from God, but questions often filled with irony and divine firmness, even if God does not put them to him in a cruel way.

God's questions cover three critical areas:

1. The first area includes Job's unfair criticisms which darkened, rather than shed light on God's

plans (38:4-38). Job had badly misrepresented God's wisdom as it is seen in God's creating the universe (38:4-7), including questions about cosmology (38:4-7), oceanography (8-11), meteorology (34-38), astronomy (31-33), and zoology (39-41).

2. The second area in which God continues to quiz Job is his inability to explain why ten selected beasts and birds (except the horse,[1] 39:19-25) were all undomesticated: The lion (39-40), the raven (41), mountain goat (39:1-4), deer (39:1-4), wild donkey (39;5-8), ox (9-12), ostrich (13-18), hawk (26), and eagle (27-30).

3. Finally, in the third area where God questions Job, it is about the efforts Job has made to restrain the forces of evil in this world (40:1-41:34).

God appears to have introduced these questions to determine Job's competence to stand trial. Job might be able, perhaps, to answer some of the simple questions about the earth and its origins, but would he not be deficient in many other areas? Let us look first at the easier questions God uses to help Job see himself for what he is.

1. Where were you when I laid the earth's foundation? Tell me if you understand (38:4).
2. Who marked off its [the earth's] dimensions? Surely you know! (38:5a)
3. Who stretched a measuring line across it [the earth]? (38:5b)

---

1. See 'Horses.' Edwin M. Yamauchi, *Dictionary of Daily Life in Biblical and Post-Biblical Antiquity,* (Hendrickson Publishers, Massachusetts, 2016).

4. On what were its [earth's] footings set,

5. Or who laid its [the earth's] cornerstone (38:6)
   While the morning stars sang together
   And all the angels shouted for joy? (38:7)

God uses this metaphorical language to address Job, for in this series of five questions, God uses poetry to describe how the earth was built on a foundation that had a cornerstone with a place that had real dimensions that were marked out by God the Master Designer of the universe. William Henry Green describes the chapters of Job 38-42 as 'beyond all comparison the most sublime portion of this wonderful book [of Job].'[2] Green goes on to add, '[God] has no intention [however] of placing Himself at the judicial bar of His creatures, and erecting them into judges of His conduct.'[3] Job must show more respect than his words at times seemed to measure up to.

Ever since we heard the speeches of Elihu, who was the youngest of the four so-called 'comforters' of Job, we came to expect that Yahweh Himself would come to address Job, for that is what Elihu had hinted would happen in his speeches. It is for this reason that we come to some of the most sublime teaching in the book of Job, even though there have been, at times in the previous discourses of this book, some searching and uplifting thoughts marked with supreme beauty and force. But the words of Yahweh are marked with a grandeur and a majesty which is appropriate to deity alone.

---

2. William Henry Green, *The Argument of the Book of Job Unfolded* 1874 reprint, (Minneapolis: James & Klock, 1977), p 285.

3. Ibid., p. 286.

Here finally, is Job's big moment – he gets his audience now with God! He had, however, worried a bit about appearing in court before God, for he feared that such terror would overtake him that it would intimidate him, and thus, he would not be able to frame his questions adequately for God (9:34; 13:21). Still, Job looked forward to such a face-to-face encounter with God and a meeting with Him where he could personally ask God why he was suffering so much (13:15, 20, 24). If that had not been possible, then Job wished (as an alternative plan) that God would put into writing why He had singled him out for such misery (31:35 -37). But Elihu had warned Job that such a request that set the time for their litigation was not proper for a mortal (34:23). However, Job would not be denied his request.

But it must be stressed once again that God will not allow Himself to be put in the witness-dock at the whim or pleasure of His creatures with demands that He justify His actions towards them. Mortals have no right to censure God or His ways, for as sovereign Lord He moves in an altogether different plane and He is accountable to no one but to Himself.

In the meantime, Job has been subjected to unremitting assaults by Satan. But as the Lord had predicted, Job had withstood all Satan's attacks, even though the accuser of the brethren, Satan himself, had done everything in his power to get Job to curse God and to forsake Him. Thus, none of Satan's attacks had been effective in detracting Job from his fear of God and his refusal to curse God.

God begins His questioning of Job in 38:1 by announcing his name as 'Yahweh,' not His generic name of 'El' or

'Eloah,' which was used by the other speakers in this book. His question is this: Who is it that dares to obscure the divine plan or purpose with words that are so devoid of understanding, if not in respect for God Himself? So, Job had better prepare himself, for he is now going to get what he asked for; all we can hope for is that he is prepared for what is going to come his way!

1. WERE ANY MORTALS (SUCH AS YOU) PRESENT WHEN GOD LAID THE FOUNDATIONS OF THE WORLD (38:4-7)?

Our Lord uses more than irony as He asks if Job had been around to assist Him when He 'laid the earth's foundations?' (38:4). Job had not even been born as yet, so how could he have been of any help to God in His mammoth project of laying the foundations for the universe? The Lord depicts the creation of the earth as the construction of a building that had footers for its foundations, dimensions that had to be measured out, with pillars that had to be set and a cornerstone prepared to cap it all off. The question for Job is this: Where were you Job, when I did all of this?

This is a question that brings Job's ignorance and insignificance right up to the surface. Job of course, knows that God created the universe, but his knowledge of this fact is not from personal observation. Therefore, it was impossible for Job to claim that he had given any type of advice on such a huge project to Yahweh. But that raises another point, if Job had been deficient on how the earth came to be, how could he possibly think he could advise God now on how to govern the earth? To be short in the former area was to be short in the area of governance as well!

When God built the earth, His work was accompanied by a lot of singing and joy (38:7). For instance, the 'morning stars,' which may be another name for the 'sons of God,' God's angels and His heavenly hosts, boldly sang out His praise as the work progressed. In fact, in Psalm 148:2-3, the stars and angels are mentioned together in their joyous task of praising the Lord at the creation.

2. WERE ANY MORTALS (SUCH AS YOU) HELPING GOD GATHER THE SEA TOGETHER AS IT CAME INTO BEING (38:8-11)?

Yahweh moves to this second level of questioning, asking if Job, or any mortal he knows, had helped Him with constructing the seas and setting the boundaries for the waters? (38:8). Does Job have any idea, or which mortal it was, who built hedges and set up boundaries so that the oceans and their waves did not overwhelm the dry lands (10)?

The sea was not God's adversary, as the sea so frequently appears in Mesopotamian and Ugaritic mythology, but it is described as a newborn baby, who was conceived behind the doors of the womb and wrapped in a blanket of clouds and thick darkness. Thus in verse 8 the Lord mixes the metaphor where the raging waters are pictured as bursting forth from the womb and which needed to be restrained by doors, just as the earth's shorelines were viewed here as having gates that held the water back like a dam on its shores (11, cf Jer. 5:22).

But once again, Job had nothing to do with God's work in building the sea; God had done it all by Himself without Job's help!

3. WERE ANY MORTALS (SUCH AS YOU) INVOLVED IN CREATING LIGHT FOR THE EARTH (38:12-15, 19-21)?

From the creation narrative in Genesis 1 we know that God made two great lights for the earth; the greater one was to rule the day and the lesser one was to rule the night (Gen. 1:16). It must be carefully noted, however, how the writer of the Genesis account purposefully avoided using the Hebrew names for the 'sun' (Hebrew *shemesh*) and the name for the 'moon' (Hebrew *yeraach*), so as not to be guilty of making the sun and the moon into idols or gods that were to be worshiped.

Job is pointedly asked, if had ever told the dawn to get to its post? (38:12). Such a question is filled with irony, for mortals cannot command the sun to shine in the morning, or the moon to rise at night. Even the wicked doers of evil are smart enough to know that when the sun comes up in the morning, it is best if they run for cover in a hiding place, just as cockroaches run for cover when the lights in an infested room are suddenly turned on.

Even the 'upraised arm' (15), which like the clenched fist shaken against its foes accompanied by a bent arm, called elsewhere the 'high hand' in Hebrew, represented a defiance and arrogance against God. However, when the light of dawn appeared, all the signs of rebellion against God stole away into the shadows.

The Lord personifies light and darkness as He asks Job if he knows where either of these two lights live? (19) These are the first two of five questions put to Job about light and darkness. God also asks Job if he was able to take the Lord to their places? Did Job know what paths to take to get to the abodes of light or darkness? (20). Then with a note of sarcasm, the Lord adds in words similar to these: 'Since you are one of the oldest men of this community, (Job could have been around only 120 years old at the time), you must have been around at creation too!' But that makes the point in a most dramatic way, for what was the brief lifetime of Job in comparison to God's ancient work in creation? Job is being reduced to silence, and he is being treated to a lesson in how little he knows in comparison to his audacious claims in the past.

4. HAS JOB (OR ANY OF YOU MORTALS) JOURNEYED TO THE UNDERWORLD (38:16-18)?

God has another five questions for Job that cover things Job has never seen, much less understood. Has Job been to the 'springs of the sea?' (16a)? Has he ever gone to 'the recesses of the deep' (16b)? Has he been shown the 'gates of death' (17)? Has Job been shown the 'gates of the shadow of death' (17b)? What about the width of the earth? Do you Job know what that is all about (18a)?

All of this is clearly off limits to Job and to mortals similar to himself. So, who is this mortal that is making all the fuss about an appointment with God? Job knows so little about God and the vastness of His work and knowledge that it is pathetic to even think about all the racket and noise this one mortal has made about his being given a bad hand and a poor shake. Who does he think he is?

5. Do any mortals (such as you) understand the power and mystery of the storm, the stars, or the clouds (38:22-38)?

Yahweh gives one of His longest speeches in this section (22-33) as he calls Job's attention to His divine use of the storm in all of its power, mystery, and unpredictability. Previously, both Elihu (37:1-13) and Job himself (6:16; 28:26) had pointed to the effectiveness of the storm, as could be seen in the effects caused by its lightning and thunder, not to mention the effects left by the snow and the ice.

Each element in the storms and in the weather-patterns on earth were given a special role to play by the Lord. To begin with, the words 'storehouses' (or 'treasuries') are better rendered 'arsenal' as it is already rendered in Jeremiah 50:25. Thus, God keeps in storehouse the rain, the snow, and the hail to be used as His weapons when needed. Thus, it would happen, in later history, for example, that God would send His reserve of hail in the seventh plague on Pharaoh and Egypt (Exod. 9:22-26) as He did when He rained hail down on the fleeing Amorites in Joshua's conquest of the land of Canaan, so that more died of the hailstones, than perished from the onslaught of Joshua and his troops (Josh. 10:11). Moreover, in the last days the Lord will use hail once again, only this time

He will send one hundred pound hailstones to fall on humanity as the plague of the seventh angel will pour out God's wrath in Revelation 16:21.

It was about this phenomenon that God asks Job, Have you been to my heavenly arsenals and seen what I have stored up in those warehouses? (22). I have reserved the stock in these warehouses for 'times of trouble' and 'for days of war and battle' (23). So, Job if you have not seen those arsenals, have you made your way 'to the place where the lightning is dispersed' (24a)? What about the place from which I scatter 'the east winds?' Have you been there and seen any of that? (24b). What about the torrents of rain that I send on parts of the earth and how they 'cut a channel' through the land? (25a). Have you seen any of that work of mine Job? What about the routes my thunderstorms have taken in a storm? Have you seen any of that Job? (25b).

There is so much that we mortals are totally ignorant about. For example, why does God allow rain to fall in the desert where few if any people live and where so few, if any, are able to profit from the watering of such dry land (26)? But on the other hand, we must not think that we know where all of that water will eventually end up; it may end up in a spring, or an oasis, miles away from where the rain fell. That is something that is to be left with God and not for we mortals to fuss about.

There is so much Job just does not know. Again Job is ignorant of the origin of rain, dew, ice, and frost. (28-30), Once more, to teach Job, God uses the poetic figure of childbirth as He had in 38:9, only this time God asks Job if the rain has a father? (28a). Or what about this question

Job? Who gave birth to things like the dew, ice, or frost? Only God could change liquid substances into the stone-like hardness of ice and huge hailstones (30).

But then God takes His student Job into the celestial realms where the constellation creations of God called Pleiades, Orion, and the Bear (= the Big Dipper) reside (31-32). Does Job know 'the laws of the heavens' (33a), or how the cluster of stars in the constellations are held together? (32). Once again, Job is left speechless, for he knows nothing about 'the ordinances of the heavens,' or how the sun, moon and stars are all governed, much less how they began (33). Job is personally unable by raising his voice to command the clouds to produce rain or to instruct the lightning bolts where they must go in all their brilliance (35).

6. Have any mortals (such as you Job) assisted God in the creation of animals (38:39–39:30)?

Of this section beginning with verse 39, Robert Alden commented,

> 'God took Job on a guided tour of his menagerie, point-ing [out] to him those species that were especially wild, rare, or remote. The questions continue, not to demean Job, but to glorify God.'[4]

God begins with the lion first of all, for here is the king of the beasts. But it was not Job who had instructed the king of beasts to hunt for its prey; no, it was God who taught this animal how to crouch down in his den or 'lie

---

4. Alden, p. 381.

in wait in the thicket' (40). It is in just the same way that God provides for the raven, when its young cry out to God for food (41). Notice that the young ravens 'wander about for the lack of food' (41c), because their parents did not supply them with food, thus if God had not taught them their behavioral traits, they would have perished from lack of food.

Job did not have a clue about when or where the mountain goats that roamed En Gedi ('Spring of the Goats') in Israel gave birth (39:1-4). Rarely did these elusive animals of the rocky terrain give away the place where they would give birth to their young or the duration of their gestation period. But it seemed that no sooner had they crouched down and brought forth their young and the labor pains were over, then the next thing seemed to be their offspring grew strong and off they bounded without returning (39:3-4). Job had not provided the mechanisms for their life cycle, but it was God alone!

God is not finished with Job yet, for if he still wants time for an interview with God, there are some more questions for him before that interview could be observed. In verses 5-8, God wants Job to tell Him who had untied the ropes on the wild donkey and let him go free (5). The answer was it was God who had set the wild donkey free, not Job. To capture the humor of all of this, God asks Job, 'Can you picture the wild donkey in an urban setting with all of the noise and commotion of urban areas, and hear its owners trying to give this animal orders under that cacophony of noise?' (7).

God asks Job seven more questions in verses 9-12 as He inquires what he knows about the wild ox. Here is an animal that also has a will of its own and is most difficult to domesticate and tame for use on the farm. This large bovine animal, with its pointed horns, was not open to giving up its freedom easily, for it disliked the harness used to plow and disc the land (10). This animal's strength had to be guarded against, for it could turn just as easily and ferociously harm the tamer trying to tame it and seriously injure or kill that farmer as it could be used to till or harrow the soil.

Included in God's menagerie of animals is one of the silliest of all, the ostrich (13-18). This time, instead of asking questions of Job, perhaps it is also a moment for comic relief. God may have made the ostrich for His joy and entertainment, for this huge, lanky bird is known for its speed as well as for its stupidity. It produces thick-shelled eggs which it deposits in the sand and then abandons almost as if in an absent-minded way (15). The ostrich would not get the 'Mother of the Year' award, for she treats her young harshly 'as if they were not hers' (16a). God just did not give her wisdom, or even a good share of old-fashioned common-sense (17). But put the ostrich in a race with a horse and she will reach speeds of forty miles an hour (18).

This observation raises the topic of horses in verses 19-25. But once again Job can make no claim to contributing or knowing things about a horse. Job contributed nothing to the horse's strength, its flowing mane, or its ability to leap over hurdles or fences. This animal is afraid of nothing (22) and it loves to enter into battle up against the sword (25). But Job had made no contributions in the area of the horse's origins or development either!

Finally, Yahweh points Job to look at the hawk/falcon (or even 'harrier') and the eagle (26-30). What the lion is as king of the beasts, so these two birds are kings of the avian realm. Here again the eagle is a creation of God that is known for its strength, its speed, and its ability to spot prey at an enormous distance away. Here too Job had nothing to contribute.

So, the first level of questions from Yahweh in part I comes to an end in 39:30. God's interrogations have ranged from the creation of the cosmos to His providential building and making of the king of the beasts and the king of the avian realm. By this time, Job is no longer as cocksure as he once had been, when he repeatedly sought for his interview with God. In fact, he must have felt downright stupid by this time. His own case now seems to have been dwarfed into insignificance in the face of the magnificence and awesomeness of the Creator of everything.

Conclusions

1. Yahweh's wisdom easily exceeds that of Job or of any other mortal. God showed Job things he had never even dreamed about. Did that help Job and his request for an interview with God?

2. In a pattern which aimed at teaching Job a thing or two, God took Job round and round in His creation to display His handiwork and to reduce him to silence and to appropriately humble him before God. Did it work?

3. For the first time, Job realizes that he has gone too far in his protest against God. It had been wrong and downright brash of him to fault God with injustice.

4. There was only one thing left for Job and that was to confess: 'I am unworthy ... I have no answer ... I will say no more' (40:4-5).

QUESTIONS FOR REFLECTION
AND DISCUSSION

1. Why did God urge Job to 'gird up the loins of his mind' if he was going to answer the Lord? What did that mean?

2. How did Yahweh's discussion on creation relate to Job's problem of suffering, if at all? What was God's point if He did not directly address Job's immediate problem?

3. How did God reduce the man from Uz to silence when He questioned him about the creation of the animal world (38:39–39:30)?

4. Discuss the nature of the wide-ranging topics Yahweh introduced and what did they tell us about how God made and governed the world? How did His governing the world fit with His helping mortals with their struggle with pain and sickness?

5. Why is it important to note that the morning stars sang as the foundations of the earth were being set up?

6. What point does God make about His formation of the constellations? How does that apply to Job's problem?

Chapter 12:
Job 40:1–42:17

God challenges Job:
Part 2

'The LORD blessed the latter part of Job's life
more than the first' (Job 42:12).

INTRODUCTION: YAHWEH'S SECOND SPEECH – 40:1-5

Yahweh begins His second speech, or part 2 of His
thorough interrogation of Job, with questions aimed at
getting Job's mind in the right perspective. The Lord gets
right down to business as He bluntly asks:

> Will the one who contends with the Almighty, correct
> him: Let him who accuses God answer him. (v. 2)

By now Job must be thoroughly worn out with all the
dialogue back and forth, and now the hard questioning
by God. His mind must surely be swirling with all
that he had been shown by his Redeemer and his own
absolute ignorance of any of what he was being quizzed
on. I think he may have decided by now that he had no
right to accuse God of being unfair or unjust – it was
just plain stupid on his part in fact, he replies with these
words of concession:

> I am unworthy – how can I reply to you? I put my hand over my mouth. I spoke once, but I have no answer- twice, but I will say no more (40:4-5)

The display of Yahweh's wisdom in His work of creation has forced Job to conclude that this is just a huge mismatch between himself and the Lord. Job's puny wisdom was not in the same league as the Creator of the universe. Previously, Job had boasted that if he ever was given an audience with God, he would give an account of his every step and he would approach Him like a prince (31:37). These huge assertions vent bold bravado, but now Job does not see himself in any match with God, for he now feels that he should have kept his mouth shut! And even though he is now silenced before God, it does not seem as if he has learned all that God has for him to learn as yet. Therefore, it will be necessary for God to take Job deeper into an understanding of His purposes and His will. Yes, Job must go still deeper into the knowledge of God and His nature. Too often, that is exactly where we are left standing with all of our questions about suffering! But God still has more for Job!

Once again, as in 38:3, Job is told to 'brace [himself] like a man' (40:7) for God wants to question him further. Already Yahweh has given Job a wide-ranging tour of the universe and the animal world in 38:4–39:30. He has shown Job that in accusing God of unfairness he has challenged the One who is the source of all wisdom, knowledge and power. He has shown Job that it is best for him to just shut his mouth and answer nothing! Now God will speak to Job out of the swirling wind coming in the approaching storm (40:6).

1. YAHWEH'S SECOND SPEECH (40:1–41:34)

A. Does Job want to take over God's job? (40:1-14)
The Lord will use the same pattern of questioning that He used in the first part of His address to Job (38:1–39:30), which covered the two areas of creation, namely, the inanimate and the three animate realms of creation. But in this, His second questioning of Job, God will turn to two of the larger animals of creation: the Behemoth and the Leviathan. Here were two awesome critters and as hard to manage as one could ever imagine.

Once again God would speak to Job in the midst of a storm just as He had in 38:1 – from the 'whirlwind' of the stormy and cloudy heavens. He again calls upon Job to 'gird up the loins of his mind' as he had in 38:3, for Job would be facing some pretty severe and tough questioning under the precise probing of the Lord! God would pose the questions and Job would presumably give the answers – that is, if he had any at all to give (40:7b-c)!

God had not forgotten the subject that Job kept insisting upon – it was the subject of God's fairness. But Job wanted to raise this question as a basis for condemning God's justice, for he felt he had been unfairly picked on. So the Lord puts the question directly to Job:

> Would you discredit my justice? Would you condemn me to justify yourself? (40:8)

Job has gone to such lengths in his attempt to justify himself that he finds himself accusing God of faults and errors! That is why God follows his charge immediately with His own dramatic question to Job:

> Do you have an arm like God's and can you voice thunder like his? (40:9)

Job is not at all God's equal, nor is he anywhere near to being in the same league as God, neither is he God's superior! He is only a mortal. The Bible uses the metaphor of God's 'arm' as a biblical symbol for 'strength.' In no sense does Job, or for that matter, any other mortal, even come close to measuring up to God's power or His justice. If Job was that far off center in his thinking, and if by so doing, he was attempting to play God, then let him play the part fully. Let him, God instructs him sarcastically, adorn himself with glory, splendor, majesty and honor, just as God Himself possesses, and show himself to be supreme over all (40:10). After Job has sort of dressed for the part of taking God's place, his first assignment is to take on the proud and the wicked as he unleashed the fury of his wrath, as he was going to bring them down low (40:11). Moreover, Job was to humble every proud man and crush the wicked person right where they were standing (12). Job was to end this charade by burying all of these wicked creeps in their graves as he shrouded their faces in the grave as well (13). If Job could carry out these administrative duties, ones that he had charged God with neglecting, then God would concede the point to Job, that he was superior himself, and that Job could save himself by his own right hand (14). But if Job could indeed take over for God, then why would he be praying for a Mediator, or an Umpire, to go between himself and this wicked world scene (9:33)? He was all he needed; he would be his own savior! But Job is a mere mortal, not a God! So it is impossible for him to take over for God!

B. Is your strength, Job, like that of the Behemoth I made (40:15-24)?

God focuses on two animals, the one considered by some to be one of the strongest land animals (40:15-24), and the other one of the wildest and most vicious of the sea animals (41).[1] The point of God's questioning is the same as it was in the first part of His speech: that is to show Job how ignorant in knowledge, puny in strength, and over-all-deficient in everything he is in comparison to God. This aim is clearly voiced by our Lord in 41:10b-11a:

> Who then is able to stand against me? Who has a claim against me that I must pay?

Whether these animals are actual living creatures or whether they were mythological allusions to Near Eastern gods and the like, is variously stated by different scholars. However, both Behemoth and Leviathan are declared to be made by God (40:15 and Ps. 104:26b). Moreover, the scriptural reference to the distinctive parts of the anatomy of both animals also argues for their being real creatures made by God rather than for their being mythological references. This does not mean that there are no figurative

---

1. See 'Wild Animals and Hunting.' Edwin M. Yamauchi, *Dictionary of Daily Life in Biblical and Post-Biblical Antiquity,* (Hendrickson Publishers, Massachusetts, 2016).

or poetical features that are used to describe these real animals in this text – there are the seven heads of Leviathan, or the smoke that comes from Leviathan's nostrils, or the fire that comes from his mouth. These may indeed be figurative exaggerations with the aim of communicating in the poetical forms used as part of this genre, yet they still are describing real animals.

The word 'Behemoth' is the plural Hebrew word for 'beasts' but since the word refers here to a single animal, the plural rendering of the word probably points to the animal's strength. Various suggestions as to the identity of this Behemoth are: an elephant, because its tail is like a cedar tree (40:17), or an extinct hornless rhinoceros, a plant-eating brontosaurus dinosaur, because of its massive body strength and tail like a cedar tree, a water buffalo, because of its habitat in the marshes, or what is most likely, a hippopotamus – an animal which was known to ancient Near Eastern cultures and to Egyptian records as one that was often hunted with harpoons and barbed hooks.

But Behemoth was made by God (40:15b). It fed on grass like an ox (15c) and had overwhelming strength (16-18) with power in the muscles of its belly (16b) and a tail that when swung was like a cedar tree being tossed about (17a). The sinews of its thighs were close knit (17b), and it had bones that were like tubes of bronze (18a), with limbs that were like rods of iron (18b). Here was an animal that was not easily trapped, for often his eyes and nose were the only parts of his body that protruded out of the water as it swam along the bodies of water, making him most slippery to catch or handle (24).

So Job, the Lord urges, take a good look at the Behemoth! If it is a hippopotamus, then it weighed something like 8,000 pounds! It is said that it 'ranks first among the works of God, yet his Maker can approach him with his sword' (19). What about you, Job? Do you want to take up the task of subduing this animal? You had better be careful, for you do not know what you are getting into. Your strength does not equal or match this animal's strength. No one could capture this huge land animal 'by the eyes' or 'pierce his nose' for as already noted here, its eyes and nose were the only two parts of this behemoth that protruded out of the water as he glided along through the swamps and marshes (40:24). With only those small parts of his massive body available for grasping, how did Job propose to capture it? Job has no reply or answer for the Lord! So Job just keeps his mouth shut!

C. Can you, Job, pull in Leviathan with a fishhook? (41:1-11)
Next our Lord turns to Leviathan and asks Job if he could pull this sea creature into his captivity 'with a fishhook'? (41:1). Many think this Leviathan might be a crocodile or an alligator, but there is little certainty that this identification is the correct one. It too is an amphibious animal, as was behemoth, living in the marshes and rivers, and generally huge in size. It too was really tough to catch, for its skin also made it difficult for man's weapons to penetrate. Therefore, it too, like the behemoth, was deeply dreaded by mortals.

The first eleven verses of Job 41 focus on how difficult it would be to capture Leviathan with ordinary fishing equipment. In fact this section of the chapter ends like the following two sections, each with a note about how frightened men were by this animal (41:9-11; 25, 33-34).

Our Lord uses still more questions as He interrogates Job further on how to capture this Leviathan. Here is a list of the questions found in verses 1-8:

1. Can you, Job, pull Leviathan in with a fishhook?
2. Can you, Job, tie down his tongue with a rope?
3. Can you, Job, put a cord through his nose?
4. Can you, Job, pierce his jaw with a hook?
5. Will he keep begging you, Job, for mercy?
6. Will he speak to you, Job, with gentle words?
7. Will he make an agreement with you, Job?
8. Can you, Job, make him your slave for life?
9. Can you, Job, make a pet out of him like you can make a bird a pet?
10. Can you, Job, put him on a leash for your girls?
11. Will traders barter for him?
12. Will you, Job, divide him up among the merchants?
13. Can you, Job, fill his hide with harpoons?
14. Can you, Job, fill his head with fishing spears?
15. Do you think, Job, you will ever forget it if you lay a hand on him?

The Lord humorously warns Job that if he tries some of these stunts with this animal he would never do it again (41:8). This was one fierce reptile. And any hope of ever capturing him was just way outside any thinking man's list of possibilities. Here was one creature you just did not arouse or awaken (10). Consequently, if no one could successfully take on this supposed crocodile, then why on earth would a mere mortal think that he could take on God? Job has still more to learn, despite all that he has achieved up to this point, for he has to trust the Maker and Builder of the universe. If he has been slow to receive the words of instruction, then the lesson of this terrifying crocodile has to be another way to learn the lesson.

D. Job, can you learn anything from the Leviathan's anatomy (41:12-25)?

God goes on to talk about Leviathan's limbs, strength, and graceful form (12), which lead to some more questions for Job in verses 13-14:

1. Who, Job, can strip off the outer coat of the Leviathan?
2. Who, Job, will approach this reptile with a bridle?
3. Who, Job, dares to open Leviathan's jaws with their bare hands?
4. Who, Job, dares to open his mouth with all its fearsome teeth?

Leviathan had thick scales that were like a human warrior in full metal armor. His skin was so thick and so closely put together that it appeared impenetrable (13). This animal was just as famous for his long jaws that could hardly be pried open by a mortal's hands, and his huge sharp teeth which must be avoided at all costs. (14)

The scales of Leviathan were positioned close together so that his back had as it were rows of shields that were tightly sealed together (15-17). Even the sneeze of this crocodile 'threw out flashes of light', as the spray from his nostrils left the appearance of a flash of light in the atmosphere (18a). His eyes, which protruded out of the water as he moved through the current, were like the 'eyelids of the morning' (18b), for as the crocodile emerged from the water, his pupils grew larger and larger just like the rays of the sun enlarged on the horizon. It should be noted that even in the Egyptian hieroglyphics the eye of the crocodile represented the 'dawn'.[2]

The crocodile's pent-up breath once added to the water in his mouth, formed a stream that belched forth from his mouth leaving what appeared to be a stream of fire in the sunshine (19-21). The strength of his neck was another reason to fear this animal (22). Similarly, his flesh was tough and firmly stretched over his body (23). His chest was as 'hard as a rock, [indeed] hard as a lower millstone' (24). With a description of this animal like this, it is no wonder that as this alleged crocodile emerged from the water, even those who claimed to be the strongest among mortals were terrified by the presence of this animal (25).

E. Job, can you capture this animal with your hunting equipment? (Job 41:26-34)
All the usual weapons of a hunter, such as the sword, spear, dart, arrows, sling stones, clubs/sabers, all were useless and to no avail in the attempt to capture this crocodile. Hunting implements made of iron and bronze, broke as easily as straw or rotten wood (26-29). The hide of a crocodile's underside is as jagged as a piece of broken pottery (30). Moreover, it is said that when this creature swims in the water, he 'stirs up the sea like a pot

---

2. Zuck, p. 182.

of ointment', or 'like a boiling caldron' (31). The wake he leaves behind his swimming pattern in the waters is so defined by the white caps it has left that one would think 'the deep had white hair' (32).

The animal is without 'equal on earth' (33a), for it is a 'creature without fear' (33b). Because he is so feared, 'He looks down on all that is haughty,' it is king over all that are proud.' (34)

2. JOB FINALLY REPLIES TO THE LORD (42:1-6)

A. It was time for Job to repent (42:1-6)
Job has been challenged by the Lord with two animals that have exhibited overwhelming strength and fierce power. It would be impossible for Job to capture or tame either of these two animals. It is for this reason, then, that Job is taught anew to respect the unmatched depth of God's wisdom, majesty, and omnipotence. This forces a concession from Job in which he says:

> I know that you [Lord] can do all things'; no plan of yours can be thwarted. You asked, 'Who is this that obscures my counsel without knowledge?' Surely I spoke of things I did not understand, things too wonderful for me to know. You said, 'Listen now, and I will speak; I will question you, and you shall answer me.' My ears had heard of you but now my eyes have seen you... Therefore I despise myself and repent in dust and ashes. (2-6)

Job has come to realize that there is too much he just has no idea of out there on earth, in the sky, and in the waters below. Job concedes that God could do anything and everything He wanted to do. No one or any power on earth could disrupt God's sovereign purpose from being carried out (42:2b). It becomes apparent to Job that any attempt on his part to question God's actions towards him or how God governs His universe was totally out of the question. Job has to admit that he has spoken out of turn in a presumptuous way about things that are just too wonderful for him and out of his depth altogether. It is time for Job to show true humility before his Lord, Maker and Redeemer!

Job once more has occasion to repeat what God had asked him when he began his speeches: 'I will question you, and you shall answer me' (38:3; 40:7). Job finally does answer God, but his answer is not as he had hoped it would be when he first began to plea for an audience and a hearing with the Lord. Instead, he quickly repents and speaks from his new insights as to who God is. It was as though he has seen God directly as compared to merely hearing about Him! Previously, he had little room in his thinking and theology for godly persons to suffer, for in his former view, such suffering was just unfair and unjust: it was a theological proposition that he felt was just untenable. But Job's view on the matter of suffering has changed. Job has gone to school with the Lord and seen some of His wisdom and power. In that display of creation and those two frightful animals, God has shown His caring and wise attention to the lower forms of His creation; now Job could begin to realize what God can and does do for mortals made in His image, like Job. Appropriately, Job retracts his poor theological talk about God and repents in dust and ashes (42:6) with the humility he should have shown to begin with. He rejects his old views forthwith and takes back all his accusations against God, for he had indulged in talk about things that were just too marvelous and too outside of his class, things that he did not know what he was talking about (42:3).

But of what, then, does Job repent? Clearly, he does not capitulate or acquiesce to the charges the Ash-Heap-Trio felt Job was guilty of. Job's clear oath of innocence in chapter 31 and God's original assessment of him in 1:1, 8 and 2-3 show that he is not suffering because he has sinned. But what Job repents of is his pride and persistent insistence that God MUST answer him and listen to his case as to why he should not be suffering. *Job sinned because he suffered*, as Roy Zuck cleverly put it, *but he did not suffer because he sinned.*[3] Elihu had warned Job that he was in deep error when he charged God with fault (33:9-13; 34:31-33; 35:2-3; 36:23). Job was to be faulted, instead of God, for his proud demands against God (32:2; 33:17; 35:12-13; 36:9; 37:24). In fact, God Himself makes the same charges against Job for Job's sheer *chutzpah* in indicting God Himself (40:2, 8). Job needs to show humility before God. Job has to ask God to forgive him of his pride and repent in humble contrition!

B. Did it turn out well for Job's three friends (42:7-9)?

Job had asked way back as he concluded his first set of responses to his three visitors, 'would it turn out well [for the three of you] if he [God] examined you?' (13:9) Actually, it has not turned out well for them as well! At least the three of them have been warned, for now as things shape up, God speaks to Eliphaz, who apparently represented the three of them, and bluntly tells them that they (the 'you' is plural in

---

3. Zuck, p. 185.

the Hebrew of 42:7) have not spoken of the Lord what was right as His servant Job has spoken (42:7)!

But what had the three of these so-called 'comforters' said about God that was incorrect? Despite the fact that the three of them had often defended God's power, wisdom, and justice in a correct way, they had incorrectly insisted over and over again that suffering from God must always be a sign that a person had sinned. They had no idea that God could use suffering to help mortals into a greater spirituality and deeper walk with Him!

However, Job never ceased maintaining that he had not sinned or that he had left any unconfessed sin standing in his life that could have been the reason for God to call down judgment on his head. Job seriously erred, however, in questioning the justice of God and in charging God with giving him what seemed like the silent treatment. Yet Job was just as insistent that to God alone belonged all power, wisdom and knowledge. Never did Job's view of God diminish or evidence a slippage from the high mark it had at the beginning of the story.

The three men of the Ash-Heap-Trio are instructed to offer a rather large burnt-offering of seven bulls and seven rams (42:8), which surely indicates how grave their error was in what they had said. Job acts as their priest, for he prays for his accusers as he helps in the offering. This also shows Job's willingness to forgive his friends, for just as he has been forgiven for maligning God's justice, so he too has to forgive. By offering their sacrifice, Job's friends are able to avoid being 'dealt with ... according to [their] folly' (42:8c).

C. What happens to Job after all of this is over (42:10-17)?
God restores to Job twice the possessions he previously had (42:10, 12), so that he 'blessed the latter part of Job's life more than the first' (42:12a). This meant that he now had fourteen thousand sheep, six thousand camels, and a thousand yoke of oxen (42:12b), double what he had previously in each case. Amazingly, his brothers and sisters, and friends who apparently had forsaken him during his troubles (19:13-14), now come to visit him, and to comfort him as 'each one gives him a piece of silver and a gold ring' (42:11). God also gives Job the same number of children he had had before, namely, seven sons and three daughters, a total of ten children (42:13). Even though the loss of the first ten children would be hard to fully replace in Job's emotions, yet God gives him ten others for his loneliness and heartache. If some think that God should have doubled this number of children as well, the point is He did, for his earlier family of ten were probably now safely in heaven so the total in this case also was twenty.

It is interesting to note that there are no names given for the seven sons but the three girls' names are given: Jemima, meaning 'dove'; Keziah, meaning 'perfume', and Keren-Happuch, meaning 'horn of eye paint', i.e. a bottle of paint used to make the eyebrows, eyelids and eyelashes more attractive (42:14). The text claims that 'nowhere in all the land were there found women as beautiful as Job's daughters' (42:15a). Moreover, Job gave these girls a physical inheritance along with their brothers (42:15b). Job also lived what some regard as twice as long after this event – 140 years (42:16) as he had lived before he faced the onslaught of these tragedies, for he lived to the age of the biblical patriarchs – as we said, perhaps to something like 210 years (42:16).

Conclusions

The Book of Job is possibly the oldest book in the Bible, and it likewise deals with one of the oldest and most challenging problems of life – the problem of suffering, pain, and tragedy in the face of the goodness of God! The whole book begins with a wager made by Satan that men serve God only because they are so blessed and favored by God. Therefore, the so-called servants of God are actually just plain selfish, for real love between mortals and God does not exist at all, implies the devil. The whole love affair between mortals and God, according to Satan, is maintained solely by God dangling rewards in front of mortals to entice them to live spiritually. If mortals keep up this reciprocal relationship, then trouble in their lives will be warded off and the alleged piety will actually be little more than a case of hypocrisy.

The fact is, however, that poor Job never knew that God had acceded to this wager with Satan and that he, Job, had been selected as God's special paragon of virtue. Nevertheless, Job steadfastly refused to curse God, no matter how much grief he faced. The devil was totally wrong in his contention that men only serve God for the rewards they get out of it. Satan learned that men can and do serve God 'for nothing' (1:9). So what are some principles we can derive from this book?

1. Job's sufferings demonstrate that mortals can serve God out of true love for Him and a desire to honor Him.

2. Job's sufferings demonstrate that pure worship is not only possible, but that such times of suffering can deepen our insight into the nature of the character and being of God.

3. Job's sufferings demonstrate that mortals can trust God even when logical explanations seem to be missing, for often we must live with mystery.

4. Job's sufferings demonstrate that God's presumed silence does not mean He is absent or unconcerned about His children.

5. Job's sufferings demonstrate that it is futile for mortals to criticize God, for there is a vast difference between God and man so that it is not possible to fully explain God, or all of His actions, to mortals.

6. Job's sufferings demonstrate that we run out of questions when we come to realize who God really is.

7. Job's sufferings demonstrate that the Most High God cannot do anything that is out of harmony with His perfection, for all that He does is right and glorious, and His way is perfect (Ps. 18:30), for our Lord is full of mercy and compassion (James 5:11).

8. Job's sufferings demonstrate that God will give to all who are hurting and grieving His grace which will be sufficient for all that they need (2 Cor. 12:9).

9. Job's sufferings and God's willingness to work through Job's lack of understanding shows that God is willing to teach us in our moments of greatest need, and despite our thick-headedness. He is teaching us to see a larger, grander view of who He is and how much He loves us. He wants His creation to have a viable, breathing, growing relationship with Him the Almighty!

QUESTIONS FOR REFLECTION
AND DISCUSSION

1. What do you think God was trying to do with Job by asking him questions about Behemoth and Leviathan?

2. What was the point of Job's contention with God and why was he so adamant about wanting to go to court with God?

3. How did Job's request get modified when he was confronted by God?

4. What is it about the character and nature of God that we miss when we fail to properly regard who God is?

5. What is your estimate of the principles we have derived from the study of Job? Which ones do you think we missed and should be added to this list?

6. After studying Job, what partial or full answers can we give to folks or to ourselves as to why persons suffer if God is so good?

7. Where were Job's brothers, sisters and acquaintances when Job was going through all of his problems?

8. How has your view of pain, suffering and grief changed as a result of this study?

Revive Us Again
by Walter C. Kaiser Jr.

In this book Dr. Walter C. Kaiser Jr. reveals spiritual principles inherent in the great awakenings of the Bible and shows us how to prepare the way for revival today. Revivals like those led by Moses and by John the Baptist provide us with clear examples of what God can do when His sovereign will is acknowledged and obeyed. Read this book and help prepare the way for revival in your community, your church and most importantly your heart.

ISBN: 978-1-85792-687-3

Coping With Change: Ecclesiastes
by Walter C. Kaiser Jr.

Ecclesiastes is a book filled with good news for those struggling
to make sense of what is happening in life. Why does man
madly pursue one thing and then another without meaning?
True joy comes from the Lord Himself, and for the one who
has learned to fear God and keep His commandments, all of
life holds purpose and delight. In *Coping with Change*, noted
theologian Walter Kaiser mines the riches of Ecclesiastes to
reveal the source of true joy.

ISBN: 978-1-78191-062-7

Grief & Pain in the Plan of God
by Walter C. Kaiser Jr.

Most of us will have faced that most delicate situation of meeting a person who is suffering. We tend to go down one of two different avenues. One is to offer well-intentioned advice – often in the form of well-worn cliches that the person will have heard several times before. The other is not to say anything at all.

Looking at the book of Lamentations Kaiser shows us how a Sovereign and Loving God can work through even the most painful moments.

ISBN: 978-1-85792-993-5

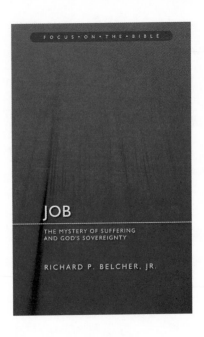

Job

by Richard P. Belcher, Jr.

Is God worthy of worship only because He blesses us? How should we respond to God when suffering comes into our lives? At the heart of the book of Job is a question about the character of God - and about how we should respond to Him. In this most recent title of the extensive Focus on the Bible series, Richard Belcher expertly deals with the difficult themes of this practical book, showing how it is still acutely applicable to the lives of believers.

ISBN: 978-1-5271-0002-2

Calvin's teaching on Job
by Derek Thomas

For many of us the book of Job stands directly in the centre of one of the most complicated problems of life – the interaction between divine sovereignty and human responsibility. Its implications for a world of suffering and injustice is one that has provoked much tortuous thought for both Calvinists and Arminians.

Calvin is still an influential theologian and was an excellent preacher. Derek Thomas uses Calvin's sermons on Job as a model for preachers today.

ISBN: 978-1-85792-922-5

Christian Focus Publications

Our mission statement —

STAYING FAITHFUL

In dependence upon God we seek to impact the world through literature faithful to His infallible Word, the Bible. Our aim is to ensure that the Lord Jesus Christ is presented as the only hope to obtain forgiveness of sin, live a useful life and look forward to heaven with Him.

Our books are published in four imprints:

CHRISTIAN
FOCUS

Popular works including biographies, commentaries, basic doctrine and Christian living.

CHRISTIAN
HERITAGE

Books representing some of the best material from the rich heritage of the church.

MENTOR

Books written at a level suitable for Bible College and seminary students, pastors, and other serious readers. The imprint includes commentaries, doctrinal studies, examination of current issues and church history.

CF4•K

Children's books for quality Bible teaching and for all age groups: Sunday school curriculum, puzzle and activity books; personal and family devotional titles, biographies and inspirational stories — because you are never too young to know Jesus!

Christian Focus Publications Ltd,
Geanies House, Fearn, Ross-shire,
IV20 1TW, Scotland, United Kingdom.
www.christianfocus.com
blog.christianfocus.com